The Wild Place

Kathryn Hulme

Plunkett Lake Press

© 1953, by Kathryn C. Hulme

Cover by Susan Erony (susanerony.com)

Praise for *The Wild Place*

"[A]n unforgettable report on the struggle, the plight, the defeat or the eventual redemption of countless victims of the time." — ***The New York Times***

"A shattering book, and one that defines, once and for all, the meaning of that ghastly twentieth-century invention, the displaced person." — ***The New Yorker***

"*The Wild Place* is a rare book — powerful and exciting, compassionate and disturbing, tragic and funny — drawn from great and strange material. It is a verbatim record of the most dramatic human debris of our time, the homeless hordes left on deposit in Germany." — ***The New Yorker***

"Little has been recorded of the heroic postwar work with masses of displaced persons, and it will be hard to find a better account than this. It is crowded with people and incidents and has a special vitality as well as the ring of truth. Highly recommended." — ***Library Journal***

"Miss Hulme's story will seize your imagination, keep you fascinated, rouse your compassion, admiration, and respect... The top book of American nonfiction published this year..." — ***San Francisco Chronicle***

"A beautiful book, heartbreaking and at the same time veined with humor. It projects the passionate sense of purpose experienced by a compassionate woman struggling desperately to salvage human lives, and it leaves us with a quickened awareness of the astounding tenacity of the human spirit, the astounding durability of hope." — ***The Atlantic Monthly***

"A sensitive and moving report, by an UNRRA field worker, of her five years' experience in European D.P. camps after the war." — ***Foreign Affairs***

"A deeply felt and deeply moving record of this whole tragedy of displacement and dispossession, this is certain to engage the heart of any reader who has one." — ***Kirkus Reviews***

To

SOLITA SOLANO

with gratitude for her help

and advice in writing this book

Foreword

They carried identity cards that designated them as belonging to no known country or continent but simply to a point on the compass. OST was printed in heavy black letters under the photograph of the bearer. OST, east. A person from the east.

There were some seven million of these compass-point citizens in Nazi Germany, working as slave laborers in the plane and ball-bearing factories, in the textile mills and mines, in the sugar beet and cabbage fields, and all the registered slaves carried these peculiar passports naming OST as their place of origin. Whenever the Nazi guards demanded a show of identification, they undoubtedly looked at that single word OST and felt that in one way most certainly their Führer's mystical *Drang nach Osten* had paid off well. The only ones who did not carry such cards were those behind the barbed wire of the concentration camps: their only identification was a number branded or tattooed on the inside of the right arm.

When this vast population of slaves was uncovered by the Allied armies in 1945, they had been OST people for nearly six years, ever since the first Nazi blitz into Poland and the later thrusts onward and eastward through the Ukraine and up as far as the little Balt republics of Estonia, Latvia and Lithuania, which stood then like outposts of democracy only some three hundred miles from Leningrad and facing out toward Sweden across the Baltic Sea. Since the majority of them had been brought into Germany as war plunder and obviously had to have come from somewhere more specific than a direction in space, the Allies invented a new name for the OST people, indicating their state of being rather than a generalized place of origin. They were named Displaced Persons.

Smoke was still curling from the blasted ruins of a vanquished Germany when the first relief teams of UNRRA (United Nations Relief and Rehabilitation Administration) were probing the desolation in search of this new kind of debris of modern war, the displaced ones, of whom the Army had managed to dispatch almost five million back to their homelands, leaving the remainder to be found, counted and cared for. These had been rounded up under whatever roofs had been left intact, usually under the roofs of the great Wehrmacht barracks, which had been as ubiquitous as railroad stations throughout the land, but which, unlike the stations, had been occasionally skipped over by the Allied precision bombers, probably on foresighted orders.

Like the displaced persons assigned to their care, the relief teams were themselves a new phenomenon. The teams were made up of nationals from many of the Allied countries and they were, in a sense, the United Nations in a test tube: small groups of a dozen or so representing five or six different countries, not sitting in diplomatic politeness around some international round table with earphones at each place to give simultaneous translations, but thrown off into the wilderness of World War II's destruction like small wandering tribes from Babel, to live together all twenty-four hours around the clock with no escape in any direction, to break bread together three times daily and to do a work that had never been done before. And, in the beginning, with not much more to do it with than the two hands, the smile and the trust in God which each one took to the field as basic equipment.

This is the story of one small part of that immense experiment described by Roosevelt at the round table conference that created UNRRA — "As in most of the complex and difficult things in life, nations will learn to work together only by actually working together." It is a story of the small part played by just one group of people in the United States Zone of Occupation in Germany, in the strange half-world of the DP camps, where two million of Europe's uprooted lived bracketed between two liberations — the first from the Nazis in 1945, and the second from the camps themselves, anywhere from 1947 until 1952, when the final families acceptable for emigration elsewhere were safely salvaged at last.

During those years until the first emigration doors opened, which seemed somehow to be outside of time, what you really were watching was the slow stumbling progress of a world learning how to become its brother's keeper; but you could not know that then. You were down in the eventful grassroots. Closed away from that outside world as effectively as if you inhabited a small planet adrift from earth like a raft in space, you knew only the queer inverted life of the DP camps, which had to be learned step by step because never before had anything quite like it been even imagined — except possibly by the artist who painted the Sistine's "Last Judgment," or by the author of *Alice in Wonderland.*

~ 1 ~

We began by being lost in the middle of a German forest on a night in late July, 1945, an UNRRA field team in search of its mission, twelve persons speaking five languages among them; but only the small red shoulder patches stitched to our uniform sleeves showed at that moment that we belonged together and had a common aim.

Grumbling in French, Dutch, Norwegian, Flemish and English, we hardly sounded like the embodiment of a noble dream of international co-operation as we climbed stiffly down from our two antique Army trucks to gaze at another unmarked fork dimly illumined by defective headlights. For twelve days we had been crawling from the UNRRA base camp on the Cherbourg peninsula toward this spot in a Bavarian forest that looked like the nether side of nowhere. Our international indoctrination had lasted all across France, but once we crossed the Rhine, the ruptured roads of Germany seemed to have jolted it out of us. You could feel national antagonisms in the air.

One of the French drivers had the misfortune to speak first.

"Rien à faire," he said, just to make a human sound. "We are lost."

Expletives in five tongues answered him. The Belgian messing officer and the Corsican doctor moved in approvingly toward Pierre, the French director, to join in a Gallic chorus that named the drivers first-category cretins. The Netherlander and Norwegian warehouse and welfare officers stepped apart from where French was exploding, as from contamination. Even our supply man had a grievance to air. He was a sturdy Texan on whom I had counted to create a bloc of calm.

"Look at him," Tex drawled in disgust. "Hoppin' around like a flea on a hot stone. By God, if I have to listen to much more of that frog yakking..." He glared in exasperation at Pierre and then turned the same look on me because I spoke French and was therefore identified with the frogs.

The Belgian and French nurses glanced protectingly toward me as *"espèce de pisseuse"* rang through the clean-smelling woods. Pierre fascinated me. Now he was blaming the absent Englishwoman for our dilemma, the thirteenth member of our team, who had fallen from a truck far back in Soissons and had been left in the big white tent of an American Army field hospital. We should never have started out with thirteen. Or twelve, or fourteen...

"Now what's he rantin' about?" Tex asked sullenly.

"Just thinking out loud how we got here," I said. "Noisy nervous like always."

As if, I thought, I had known that volatile Frenchman for years instead of barely a fortnight. Twelve days in a truck had left nothing to be discovered about the man with whom I had elected to jump off into the unknown, as his deputy director. Once or twice en route, before I had got used to him, I had asked myself if this time I had let my inborn love for France carry me too far. I chose him, I said to myself. I chose him sight unseen, saying, "Team me up with a French director."

I gazed with Francophile fondness at the object of my choice venting his nerves again on the innocent drivers, his beret pushed back on his partially bald head, his broad chest bursting from the too-small battle jacket that had been issued to him back in the base camp and accepted by him with comments that had considerably limbered up my salon French. I was glad that my Frenchman had turned out to be a man as full of emotions as a Paris taxicab driver and not ashamed of a single one. Presently, just as I expected, the old *maquis* "took decision." He called the Dutch warehouse man, who spoke perfect German. They were going to look for a German farmhouse and someone who might be able to say where the refugee camp was.

"Don't stir from here, *mes enfants,*" Pierre called as he disappeared in the dark with the reluctant Dutchman. "We shall soon discover Wildflecken!"

Wildflecken! The word made magic instantly. It pulled us together from our carping national groups into a tight small circle of mutual excitement. It was a name that meant "wild place" in German, but for us it was the name of our assignment and it meant the end of wandering and wondering. We had heard the name only that morning in our Munich headquarters, a wild and lonely-sounding word not printed on any map. We had been told that Wildflecken was somewhere up in the bush beyond Bad Neustadt, in the Rhön Mountains of northeast Bavaria, that there were about two thousand DP's in the camp, and some remnants of an UNRRA spearhead team whose director had evaporated into space. Our H.Q. thought, but was not sure, that the DP's were Poles.

"Can't figure why it's not on the map," said Tex.

We had no way of knowing then that the camp we sought was within a few hundred yards of us, shrouded in the dense growth of planted pines that Hitler had used to camouflage his greatest SS training center in the whole of Germany, that the low mountains we could sense but not see rising around us had been the practice grounds for his elite ski troops when they had prepared for the attack on Russia, and that the whole locale was so secret that even its name had not been allowed to appear on any map since 1938.

"These woods would be a perfect hideout for escaped storm troopers," said our Corsican doctor, appraising the terrain with the expert eyes of the underground.

"I wouldn't mind handling a few more of those," said the Belgian messing, accenting the "more" with delicate modesty.

I looked with possessive pride at the shadowy forms clustered around. Every one of them, except Tex and me, had lived under the Nazis until only a few months ago, in occupied Belgium, Holland,

Norway and France. Even after a month's feeding on the stout American Army food of the Cherbourg base camp, the Europeans still bore marks of their years of privation. The men were lean and always hungry. The women had not yet got rid of the round podlike bellies that the war's potato diet had built out beneath their meager waistlines.

The current of expectancy made us seem nevertheless like one body waiting there in the dark, an untested, untried body with ten pairs of willing hands and the single desire to get on with a job that had to be done. Our composite character was made up of a rancher, a business-machine salesman, a skilled mechanic, a social worker, a ship's steward, an industrial accountant, two public health nurses, a specialist in contagious diseases, and myself.

Like so many unattached American women, I had done a bit of everything, including (after Pearl Harbor) a good long stint of shipyard welding which I was always sure was a compelling reason for my acceptance into UNRRA, since it proved that I was flexible. Flexibility was the key qualification for the field workers, and I knew that my comrades had all been chosen for that factor as well as I. We all leaned suddenly toward the crackle of trampled twigs that broke the silence.

Pierre's big voice bellowed ahead as he ran toward us through the trees. The quiet Dutchman got the whole story told in his own tongue to his own compatriots before our French director could put together any words that made sense.

"We're right on top of the camp," said Pierre — "just a few hundred meters beyond this fork. There's an American major..." He forgot what he was going to say about the major. He stared at us one by one like a father taking a last look at a beloved family. Then he said in a small hoarse voice: "It hasn't got two thousand... it has twenty thousand DP's. Twenty thousand Poles. *Vingt mille polonais, mes enfants,"* he repeated in French, as if he didn't believe it in English.

We climbed back into the trucks, bumped in silence over the remaining few hundred yards, drove under a wooden arch past a stone guardhouse and went into second gear. Headlights from the following truck showed we were climbing a handsomely cobbled boulevard hemmed in by tall black pines. We turned right at the first signpost we had seen since Bad Neustadt. "Florian-Geyer Strasse," it said in enameled German gothic, and underneath, on a hasty homemade arrow tacked askew: "UNRRA Billets."

Pierre looked at me with the whites of his eyes.

"They bake nine tons of bread a day in this camp," he whispered, so no one else in the truck could hear his second frightening statistic.

~ 2 ~

The major briefed us with a Brooklyn accent. He pointed his swagger stick at a German wall plan captioned "Truppenlager Wildflecken," shaped like a gigantic fan with straight roads like ribs converging on the headquarters where our offices were and curved roads swinging upward in concentric semicircles to the top of the fan, where the last arc was marked "Waldgrenze," the forest boundary line.

"You got about fifteen square miles in here, Peer... and not a foot of fence anywhere around this twenty-five-mile perimeter." The major replied to Pierre's expression with the tough tight grin of the combat man. "Security? It just ain't. You've probably got everything in this camp except Hitler and I wouldn't be surprised if you turned up that bastard when you get started on the registration. Now these squares are the blockhouses — living quarters. You've got sixty blockhouses in good shape, average three hundred and fifty persons each. Then, if you get stuck for living space, you can use the stables up here..."

"Stuck for living space?" I was multiplying sixty by three hundred and fifty.

"Sure... they're going to throw them at you fast. Army's got the idea that every Pole in Germany will fit in up here. That's why I'd take a look at those stables first thing."

"Down here are the kitchens." He swung his stick over a curved line running across the middle of the fan. "That kitchen street is one mile long, twelve kitchens, each cooking for about fifteen hundred DP's. Then up here, at the top of the camp, is the Central Supply Area. At least a dozen big warehouses. We've only emptied a couple of them. They're crammed with every damned thing you ever heard of. There's one whole warehouse full of Wehrmacht skis. You ski?" he asked me.

"I'm skiing now for the first time in my life," I said. "Go on, Major, tell us more."

"Well, over here is the place you want to look out for." He pointed to a cluster of squares outside the fanlike perimeter off in the woods to the south. "That's the bakery. Hell's Kitchen."

"Where they bake nine tons of bread a day?" Pierre sounded as if he had not yet crawled out from under that nightmare mountain of bread.

"Where they're supposed to bake nine tons a day," the major corrected. "But on any dark night you can follow the flour trail from those bakeshops through the woods into the camp, right up to the door of a blockhouse and then, if you're interested in a nice quiet little home industry, follow the flour down to the basement and see a schnapps still in action. Polish vodka. Hot stuff. Some of its blind results are lying up in these five hospitals." He pointed to five red squares scattered through the camp. "Except this one. This is the Maternity. We gave birth to about twenty-five new DP's last month and I heard we're expecting about forty-five for the month of September."

Now and again a pistol shot punctuated the briefing. The major paid no attention to these until he saw they distracted Pierre's and my attention. Then he explained matter-of-factly:

"Those are probably the Poles cleaning out their *capos,* comrades the Germans bought off and used as guards in the concentration camps. We tried to put a stop to it but it's like trying to control one of the old Wild West vigilante committees. You sure got to hand it to these Poles," he said with admiration; "they never forget."

He glanced at his wrist watch and started talking faster, covering the Polish committee that ran the camp, the DP police force that would try to run us if we didn't keep it under close control, the six hundred tons of rations that our population ate up each month, the fifteen hundred tons of potatoes we'd have to truck in and store before the first snows fell, and the thirty-six thousand cubic meters of wood we would have to get chopped, hauled and stacked before the roads iced over.

"Sure," he said, seeing us stare at the figures we were jotting down, "you've got a regular city here. Once I looked up cities around twenty thousand in the *World Almanac* just to get some ammunition for a security report I was making, asking for more men for the patrol detachment." He looked at me. "Ever been in Plattsburg, New York, or in Laramie, Wyoming, or in Modesto, California?" he asked. "Well, Wildflecken is bigger than any of those, just to give you an idea."

"Did you get your additional men?" Pierre asked.

The major burst out laughing.

"Whadda *you* think!" he exclaimed. "Army. *Army.* They're beginning to forget already that these are the little guys we fought the war for." He waved toward the office windows. Beyond, up and down the cobbled road, tramped a stream of DP's with packs on their backs, with paper suitcases stacked on small kiddy-carts that they pulled behind them, bent over low and looking at the ground. For an instant he gazed down on his little guys with a compassion so intense it had the look of anger. "There wasn't enough of the big brass around when we busted into the concentration camps and liberated some of those lousy Poles," he said in a tight harsh voice.

He pulled his overseas cap from under his shoulder strap and set it on his head at a cocky angle. You read the story of his combat life in the double row of bright striped ribbons above the left pocket of his battle jacket. From beachhead through Bulge to this little Laramie full of Poles...

"Well, I guess that's about it, Peer." He shook hands. "I've only hit the high spots but those files will fill you in. I'm leaving an officer up in Central Supply for a little while to show your man the ropes. But you won't need us very long. You'll make out OK." He gave us a leathery grin. "You pick it up fast, this DP business. Boy, do you pick it up fast."

You pick it up fast...
We picked up interpreters, we picked up cars to transport us, and Polish drivers to piece these together every time they fell apart. We picked up camp leaders, the police chiefs and the priesthood, Roman Catholic and Creek Catholic — all the people on whom we had to depend. And we picked up, in a different way, as if a new sense had sprung into operation, a troubled awareness of what it really meant to be "displaced," to have been removed abruptly and totally from your homeland, not by the hand of God but by a human conqueror in one deliberate scoop that had swept up the grannies, the babies and the cripples as well as the young and able, since slavery has no selectivity and every body that breathed was deemed fit for labor until it stopped breathing.

Some of us picked up new facial expressions as our statistics turned into people and the people turned into friends, and shortly everyone on the team had picked up an Ivan, a Zygmund, a Stanislaw or a Wasyl who became his own special DP and was loved particularly like brother or son.

And on my first day, which is the only one I can recall clearly as a unit in time with a beginning and an end to it, I picked up the job of issuing passes to DP's who needed to go out of camp. I began then by seeing the DP's one by one. The first impressions entered with such sharp shock that never again would I be able to look on a refugee mass, even in pictures, and see it collectively, see it as a homogeneous stream of unfortunate humanity that could be handled with the impersonal science of the engineer who does not ever think of the drops of water when he is controlling a flood.

Human data would be added to the years of days following that first one, but each new individual encounter would repeat the misery in a slightly different form so that you could never lump it together in convenient categories and dispose of these in one sweeping group decision. The "DP problem" was an easy generality that you had accepted until you met that problem in the grassroots and saw that it had as many faces as there were people composing it.

None of these realizations were, of course, immediately apparent. I was only glad that the major had tossed out a clue on what to do first.

"It's as good a place as any to begin," he had said at parting. "One day at this desk will add ten years to your age." And he handed over the pass job to me, including the massive German officer's desk that went with it and the interpreter who stood beside the desk.

The Countess was a tall handsome woman in her early sixties. She had the cornflower-blue eyes of the Slav and the lean *racé* face of the Polish nobility, but with all native hauteur beaten out of it by suffering so that every emotion showed instantly. I quickly learned to know in advance, by watching her face, something of the shape of the problem being unfolded to her in halting Polish, Russian, German or Ukrainian before she recited it back to me in flawless Warsaw-society French.

The major had warned me to screen pass requests carefully, weed out the black marketeers, give only where urgent and verify the need when in doubt. We never had to ask for verification; it was shown to us humbly when words failed the petitioner.

A famous tenor from the Warsaw Conservatory opened his mouth to show the broken stumps of teeth left there by a Nazi fist. He was having false teeth made by the village dentist so that maybe sometime he would be presentable to sing again. He kissed my hand when I extended it toward him with a pass, brushing his battered mouth lightly across the tips of my fingers as he murmured the polite formula *"Küss die Hand"* in the language of the people who had beaten him.

A young girl in an advanced state of pregnancy showed a note on the stationery of a tank battalion H.Q. stationed nearby. *Dear Stefania,* the note read, *Joe ain't here any more, he was transferred out last week, gone Stateside.* The girl looked at me with unbelieving eyes as she told the Countess in Polish that Joe was her fiancé, they were to be married this month, he would never have run away from her like that, without a word, without a farewell. She must talk to his friend in the battalion. There was a mistake somewhere.

A mother unwrapped a black kerchief to show us the handsome silver heirloom cup she hoped to trade with a German butcher for a few ounces of raw liver to build up her anemic child, and she lifted the child before our eyes like a lifeless white truce flag begging our mercy.

A solemn and stately little Polish boy scout stood before us with his three upraised fingers swearing fidelity to God, crown and country, a trinity of which only God remained with certainty. Then he showed us slips from his blockhouse leader recording the transfer to our camp of his mother from a Coburg camp, of his sister and brother from a French Zone camp, and now he asked permission to go forth again to seek his father, whom somebody had said that somebody had seen wandering about in the ruins of Munich. He was certain he could find his father as he had found the other members of his family scattered like leaves over the map of Germany. He had bicycled after them one by one, going forward by hunch and by hearsay from camp to camp, sustaining himself on pilfered fruit from German orchards and his passionate faith that the people who belonged to him were not dead.

The Countess knew what happened inside me when I saw my first concentration-camp brand. A little old granny neat as a bird, kerchief knotted smoothly over brushed white hair and a clean black apron tidily tied about her withered waist, told in the whispers of her native tongue that her daughter was just about coming to term in an Augsburg camp and that she must go down there to help with the birth of that grandchild whose father had died in Dachau.

"Dachau," she whispered and turned directly to me because a name like that needed no interpreter. She pushed back the full sleeve of her peasant blouse and showed me the eight numbers tattooed on the inside of her bony forearm, violet-colored against the parchmentlike skin, a row of digits separated twice by the small dashes that bookkeepers use when serial-numbering some endless project.

I saw more of them on that first day. I saw so many that I was sure my memory was branded forever and that never again would I be able to think of mankind with that certain friendly ease which characterizes Americans like a birthright.

There were two kinds of concentration-camp brands. There were the neat violet-colored tattoos running up the arm only two or three inches; then there were the ones that had been burned in with red-hot numbered irons, which took up much more skin space, running from the inside of the wrist all the way up to the inside of the elbow in a livid line of scar tissue that stood up in lumps.

The Poles did not thrust these brands at you. They revealed them only when they had no papers to authenticate some story, using them for documentation purposes only, pulling up their sleeves slowly and with an apologetic air as if reluctant to reveal to a newcomer, and an American at that, the kind of thing that went on over here before we came along.

Refugees queued up endlessly outside my office door, and each time it opened to let one out the next stepped forward fumbling wisps of paper and I thought I would drown in the stream of forlorn facts that poured over me. I had a fantastic notion that seemed momentarily very practical. If I could have been prepared for this in some way, I might not be taking it so hard. But I could not imagine what kind of preparatory course could have encompassed the endless subject of human suffering.

"I suppose one gets used to it, *enfin,*" I said.

The Countess flashed me a look that shamed me.

"But never!" she said. *"Jamais! Au grand jamais!"*

Occasionally there came a moment of relief.

An elderly man with a shock of white hair standing above a fine forehead came in with a book written in Polish. It was a monograph on the flora and fauna of Bavaria, written by a friend. The author's dedication named our applicant as a fellow botanist from the University of Cracow. All that the old professor wanted was an exit pass with no destination named, so he could wander the woodlands thereabouts and try to find some of the rare flora his friend had identified. It was difficult to tell him that the woods were off limits, that they were full of hidden stores of impounded German war matériel and that the major had ordered all DP's on pass permission to keep strictly to the main roads.

The professor silently opened his book to a floral illustration in color. He asked the Countess to read its blooming season to me — month of August only, north Bavaria, in woods above two thousand feet. While I was telling him no again, he was touching the flower print with his long delicate fingers, tracing the lilylike contour around and around.

"It's all he has left in the world," the Countess pleaded. "His entire family killed... now he has only his flowers." Her eyes forced me to pick up my rubber stamp, the seal of Wildflecken which could transform any bit of paper into a passport. On the blank line after "Destination" I wrote in "Botany" and prayed that the GI guard at the main gate was illiterate.

Once during that first day I thought of the previous night when I had stood with the team in the dark woods beyond the camp's main gate and wondered about the DP's. It seemed that I was thinking of something that had happened years ago. It seemed that these unfortunate people had always been part of my life, their myriad needs as familiar to me as if I had dealt with them always. And even then an unexpected emotion was quickening to life as the refugee stream bore toward me individuals whom I had to look at twice to make sure they were not people I had once known very well. A booted Slav looked at me with the red-rimmed eyes of my brother, the same nervous granulation of the eyelids. A shawled old lady reminded me of my mother — the same thin-veined hands of fear, the same voice when tears were near.

You're identifying, I said to myself. Better stop. *There but for the grace of God...* The new emotion stirred but did not formulate. If it had, I would have suppressed it instantly. Back there in 1945 such an idea would have been preposterous. The United Nations had just been born. We were cleaning up the human wreckage from what was most positively the last world war that mankind would allow to happen.

"This one's going to be the last today," I said to the Countess. "You look as beaten as I feel."

The young man stood before me holding a cap with a broken visor in one hand and a spray of red rambler roses in the other. He wore a strange black overcoat with moth-eaten caracul collar and khaki Army socks pulled lumpily over the ends of his trousers, long ribbed socks such as golfers wear, so that he looked sporty in a tattered sort of way. He had a tender sensitive face and neat pointed ears, over which were a few shreds of unbarbered blond hair.

"This is Ignatz," said the Countess, reading the slip he presented to her with a bow. "He desires to be your chauffeur. He is presently driving for the trucking company but desires to transfer to private service, to your service precisely."

"But I have no car yet, tell him."

Their Polish whished back and forth and I saw for the first time how laughter looked on the Countess's face. Ignatz was being quite detailed. His long capable hands described something with many parts, big, little, circular, angular, then they turned palms up, saying clearly, So there, you see?

"He has a car for you," said the Countess. "It's a wrecked Opel Kapitan which he towed in from a German garage after having examined its damages and seen that they were only exterior. He has been working on it for some time up in Central Garage. He finds nuts and bolts in the shot-up Panzer tanks lying about in the woods. He says the Opel has the best motor of any car in the garage but that no one else on the team looked at it today. Apparently, many were up there selecting cars. The director, he says, selected a car and you come next in line. He begs you to name this Opel yours and he will have it running within the week."

Before I could say yes, Ignatz went to work for me as if he knew in advance that we were going to be together for a long time and that he might as well begin to put my life in order. He removed a dusty tumbler from the desk, washed it at the sink in the corner of the office, arranged his spray of rambler roses and set it down on the desk, careful to see that it did not cover any part of the camp map or calendar under glass. He bowed deeply from the waist. Then he went out the door and firmly and efficiently dismissed the remainder of the waiting queue.

~ 3 ~

The sight of human beings crowded into cattle cars makes a singular first impression, although this sort of thing was familiar in 1914-1918 when "40 men, 8 horses," the transport slogan of Pershing's doughboys, had a racy sound to the stay-at-homes, reading about the war. Newspaper photographs showed our doughboys bunched at the wide door of the cattle car, waving like mad and grinning broadly, with one or two pointing down with a comical air at the stenciled sign on the side of the car: *40 Hommes. 8 Chevaux.*

But like everything else where humans are concerned, it is one thing to read about it and quite another to witness it, especially when women and children are looking out the cattle car doors. A sense of shame invades you. A feeling of objective guilt crystallizes and you stare at the humiliation as if you were responsible for it in some intangible fashion. The impression is unique each time. It does not seem to enter the associations the first time and then repeat afterwards with growing familiarity so that finally you accept it matter-of-factly as just one more debasement that has happened to mankind.

Within our first year in Wildflecken we were to see one hundred thousand DP's arriving and departing in cattle cars, but the first arrival from other camps in Germany, the first departure of repatriants for Poland, would not set the pattern for accustomed repetition. Each new transport was to involve us emotionally like the first.

We were not ten days on the new job when the first big incoming transport was announced. During those first days a few hundred DP's had been brought to us in Army trucks, appearing without advance warning at the main gate, and Medical had got out its DDT, Welfare had roused its billeting committee and Messing had opened up a kitchen to feed the newcomers and that was the end of it. Easy as falling off a log.

Pierre and I had explored the Wildflecken railroad station that lay like a great curved stage several hundred yards beyond the main gate, an inexplicable railhead for a village counting only some fifty peasants, a few score geese and some oxen, until you recalled that the station serviced Hitler's greatest SS camp. Its tremendous loading platform, cleanly cobbled and wide enough for trucks to back and turn, was long enough to hold forty boxcars without switching. But we were sure that no trains would be coming to us for a long time. We had followed the tracks down the valley past the little town of Brückenau, then west toward Lohr, where the railroad crossed the River Main on a viaduct arching a hundred and fifty feet above the water. We had admired the precision bombing that had cut the viaduct neatly in two.

"On sera tranquille," Pierre had said restfully, gazing up at the blasted arch.

A few days later Pierre took, over the Signal Corps field phone, the call which announced four thousand Poles were on their way to us. These spidery field phones jacketed in khaki were our only connection with the outside world, and we never knew where the calls originated or who was talking because the exchanges had code names we had not yet had time to decipher or localize. All that Pierre knew when he shouted for the Countess and me to come fast was that from Dagwood, through Blue Dog, through Red Danube, a voice had spoken.

"Four thousand, maybe more. In batches of five hundred. By rail, he said."

"By rail?" I thought Pierre was mad.

"The nearest railhead. Gemünden it sounded like." He hunted furiously over a regional wall map. "One of your cowboy colonels from Texas. What a barbarian accent." Pierre pronounced "cowboy" like a Parisian — *coo-bwah.*

"Here," said the Countess. She pointed to Gemünden, next stop beyond the bombed viaduct. "About sixty kilometers."

Pierre stared unbelievingly at the green spaces separating Wildflecken from Gemünden. Then he reached for the field phone. "Call the committee president and his billeting master. Get the team together. We need Medical, Welfare, Supply, Transport and Messing. I've got to get more trucks somewhere." He ground the handle of the field phone as if he were cranking a truck.

He got a French trucking company on temporary duty in the region. He buttered up the officer in charge with a charming peroration sprinkled with affectionate *mon vieux's* and got an entire camion company lent to us for a day.

Team members startled at the mid-morning interruption streamed into the office saying "What's up?" and the Polish committee people came in saying "We have no room" in German so everyone could understand their position immediately. They had already caught the news over the camp grapevine, that worked with the speed of light.

Pierre gave orders like a general and looked like one too, in the new officer's cap he had wheedled from an American captain. This was our first real workout as a team. I was proud of the way Pierre had boned up on all of the paperwork in the files. He knew exactly what to tell each one to do. He told Medical to make ready extra hospital beds and be at the main gate with their DDT squads to catch the trucks as they came in. Welfare likewise would be at the main gate to hand out tinned milk to children and nursing mothers. Supply would tally out five hundred rations to Messing, who would alert a kitchen for night cooking.

Then he swung on Mr. Tak Tak Schön, whose Polish committee gentry had been sitting scowling and clucking over a big ledger containing floor plans of each blockhouse. Tak Tak Schön, the president, was a merchant from Lodz who always answered *"Tak Tak,"* the Polish "yes, yes," to every question, and exclaimed *"Schön!"* in German when our plans pleased him. Nobody on the team could pronounce his Polish name so we called him by the habitual sounds he made — Tak Tak Schön.

Pierre gave him no chance to tell the Countess there was no room in the camp for four thousand more people. He stated that each of the sixty blockhouses would prepare to receive sixty-five to seventy additional Poles within the next two or three days and that if they would not move their mistresses and special-privilege people out of the private apartments they were presently spread out in, then he, the director, would do it himself and jail the block leader who failed.

Transport had its scarecrow fleet of UNRRA trucks lined up in front of headquarters by the time Pierre had finished with Tak Tak Schön. Pierre was to lead the first convoy in. Then we were all to take turns.

DP's from the camp gathered eagerly around the waiting trucks, telling drivers whom to look out for on the incoming transport. Everybody expected to have a long-lost brother, uncle or cousin turn up, or a neighbor from his own village in Poland, and you could feel the current of anticipation running from those around the trucks, through those hurrying down the cobbled hill from camp, crackling back through each forested street into the blockhouses, where the women and old folks sat like tigers at bay guarding the extra living space to which their skillfully spread trunks, crates and blanket rolls laid claim.

I saw Ignatz's black overcoat flapping through the crowd as he ran toward me with face ready for weeping. My Opel Kapitan lacked only a gasket, he said, and if he had not been fouily betrayed by a certain German mechanic who had already accepted double the amount of cigarettes required for such a gasket, he would have had the car ready for Frau Direktor. He shook with fury and shame for his unreadiness.

"Tell him never mind," I said to the Countess. "Tell him it's better anyhow I ride with the doctor. I may have to scrounge an Army ambulance for him en route."

Ignatz went to the wall map and issued instructions. His grease-blacked finger traced the thirty-five miles of winding road separating Wildflecken from the railhead.

"It's his former potato run when he was with the trucking company — Brückenau, Hammelburg, Gemünden," the Countess translated. "He says to be careful here after Hammelburg when you go through those woods. Slippery in the rain especially when catkins lie on the cobbles. Watch out for this hairpin bend in the mountains, it has a one-way bridge at the bottom."

Ignatz's finger stopped at Gemünden. He looked at the Countess with cold blue eyes, gave her a brief sharp command. For an instant I saw the Ignatz of the photograph he carried in his battered wallet. I saw a pilot of the Polish air force, the proud young face above the stiff collar of an officer's tunic with the crowned eagle of Poland embroidered on its velvet tabs.

"When you descend into Gemünden on the River Main," said the Countess in the voice of an officer, "you go into low gear. Not second, *low gear.*"

Next day at dawn I went into low gear and drove down the steep loose-graveled road into Gemünden. It was a soiled town with a few sullen Germans abroad at that hour, driving their oxcarts toward the cabbage fields. The peasants looked with disdain on the fuss we were making to receive another bunch of "dirty foreigners" and you could distinguish that phrase *"schlechte Ausländern"* in their mutterings when they had to pull to the side of the road to let our trucks go by.

The railroad station had been well bombed. Stones from blasted freight sheds cluttered the loading space so we could back up no more than six trucks at a time beside the tracks. Pierre had not said much about his transport of the previous evening, which he had managed to bring into camp before sundown. He had returned in a rage and had sat down and cranked the field phone, saying he was going to sit there until he got through channels all the way up to commanding general of American Third Army.

"You'll be there till Christmas," I said.

"Go see for yourself, *ma chère*. You'll see what I'm going to try to stop."

The doctor and I watched the empty tracks curving off into woods beyond the shattered station. Our train with an expected five hundred DP's was due. The rising sun laced the woods with thin slants of light but they had the same eerie quality as the woods of Wildflecken because there were no birds. Germany's last brutal bombings had displaced all the birds, except crows that were more omen than bird. It gave one the nervous sensation of being a deaf man among the brightening trees which ordinarily would have been alive with the dawn trills and calls of waking birds.

The strident steam whistle of the oncoming train pierced ahead through the woods. Then we saw the cattle cars dragging around the curve bringing to us the displaced who had not been able to fly out of the horror like the birds.

The cars slid slowly by us, each car door decorated with wilted boughs which framed a still life of haggard faces shawled, bonneted, turbaned, or simply wrapped around with shreds of old blanket wool, each car door framing the same tight-packed composition varied slightly here by addition of an infant at the breast, there by a crying child swung clear of the crush to ride on a man's shoulders, or at intervals by a graybeard or granny to whom chair space had been allowed in the precious footage of the open door. I stared at the composite face of human misery, unsmiling, stoic and blue with cold. Automatically I read "Pilsen" on one of the cars sliding past.

"My God, they've been at least four days in those boxcars," I said to the doctor.

"Did you count them?" he asked quickly. "I'm up to thirty-one right now."

The train ground to a stop before the last car appeared around the curve. Instantly car doors began to spew forth a gray stream from each open portal — men, women, children and gigantic bundles, young boys leaping clear and toddlers lifted down and ten-gallon soup pots, wicker baskets, perambulators, concertinas, bicycles and bedrolls mixed in with the bundled bodies issuing continuously as in old comedies of movie slapstick, but with a peristaltic rhythm as bodies and baggage momentarily cleared the car door and made space for more to surge forward from the rear corners, and even before the pulsing ceased, the mountains of luggage began piling up before each car door. Each mountain was a load for at least two trucks, not counting the gray humanity around its base.

A haggard convoy lieutenant stumbled forward from the escort car that was still out of sight beyond the bend. He thrust a bulky roster into my outstretched hand and said:

"From Pilsen. Five days en route, switching, sidetracked, changing engines, God damn these Germans. We ran out of food yesterday." His unshaved face had a drawn frantic look. "Have you got a doctor? We delivered a baby last night in car 14 and there's at least a dozen more ready to pop. Here, my man will show you."

A GI in soiled fatigues led the doctor down the rows of boxcars, pointing and talking fast as our nurses and a welfare girl came over the hill like answer to a prayer. Our Belgian driver was with them. He took command of the loading.

"Marcel," I yelled to him. "Try to segregate. Get women and children first."

"You've got about a thousand here," said the lieutenant. "At least we started out with that many but I lost some on the way. Sanitation halts. Some of 'em strayed off too far in the bushes and that damned jerry engineer refused to give more than one warning whistle, then pulled right out. One's dead. He got electrocuted." His eyes were so bloodshot you could not tell what color they were. He riveted me with a burnt-out stare. "They were running all over the cars, see? Hanging out, jumping on and off when we slowed down, climbing on roofs to grab at fresh greens to decorate those doors, and this one grabbed at a live wire overhead. He just hung there burnt to a crisp. We poked him off with a wooden pole. I think some of his family quit us at that point to stay with the body and bury it. From car 21. I made a margin note on the roster." He stopped talking. Everything had spilled out of him. He remained beside me like a sleepwalker looking at nothing.

The Belgian nurse called out that she had found someone in labor. She was helping a childlike girl into her UNRRA sedan along with a scared young man.

"Can you make it to the camp?" I cried above the din of Poles fighting to climb into the trucks and Marcel bellowing angry commands in German to let the women go first.

My voice woke the lieutenant.

"If you've got someone going on ahead," he said wearily, "you'd better warn your chief there's another thousand following behind us, about five hours behind, I think."

I had no time to scribble a note to Pierre. I gave the message orally to the Belgian nurse as her small car pulled out of the moil of roaring trucks. She nodded from the back seat, where she sat with her hand over the child-wife's belly, trying to count the frequency of the labor pains.

The Canadian nurse signaled me from a crowd of crying women near the forward end.

"I've got to take these babies on ahead," she said to me. "Make them understand. Every one I've examined so far has frightful diarrhea. Just look at that!"

She unwound a whimpering bundle and plucked open a diaper that obviously had not been changed for days. The tiny pointed buttocks lay flaming red in gray slush. "It's an outrage. They let all these mothers on the transport with no spare diapers. Two cars up there's one who speaks a little English. There was no diaper distribution. Some of them used paper when they could find any along the way." She threw the filthy diaper on the ground and shouted angrily at the mother to leave it there. "I've got to take the mothers along too, for the breast feeding. You tell those yammering husbands what I've got to do."

I started down the line haranguing the husbands in the German I had picked up by osmosis. Their anguish at even such a brief separation made me feel like a monster. They looked at me, not with belligerence but with the accumulated fright and mistrust from all the past separations they had endured which so very often had turned out to be permanent. I was just another foreigner in uniform sending their wives and babies in different directions. One hulking peasant in enormous boots and Cossack fur cap, with a child under one arm and another clinging to the edge of his sheepskin coat, just stood there and cried.

After we had segregated the ailing babies and the maternal breast that had to go forward with each, we were too worn to try further. The vast families clung together in stolid frenzy. The men swung their luggage into the trucks, piled it dangerously high above the guard rails, and then they hoisted their families on top of this, thrusting smaller members down between the cracks, kicking couchlike spaces among bedrolls for the elders, and themselves climbing atop the teetering heaps to hold these in place with straddled legs. The overloaded trucks swayed up the graveled incline and over the hill in constant procession and we held our breath for each one. Until the rain started. Then we could not bear to look any more.

The thirty-five-mile shuttle service between camp and railhead kept up all day. The French trucking company backed their sturdier trucks into the waiting ranks, but these drivers were worse than our DP drivers. The Frenchmen were making a race of it to see who could accomplish the most seventy-mile round trips before dark. We toiled at the heaped humanity and it never seemed to diminish. Sometimes in the forenoon the string of empty boxcars was pulled away and another thirty-five cars shunted into place, looking so exactly like the dawn arrival that we thought we were living a nightmare of some evil never-ending repeat pattern.

Every team member who had a car came over to the railhead and drove back emergency cases singled out by nurses and Welfare, and sometimes one handed me a progress memo from Pierre at the receiving end, and sometimes Pierre himself appeared, stripped of his bonhommie, spent and speechless. But no one on the team looked familiar as we came toward the end of that day. Not weariness but wrath had altered my teammates, a burning wordless wrath directed against nothing in sight because the population maps with the colored pins in them and the military personages who moved those pins around, trimly "consolidating" the displaced masses, were as far away as God seemed to be just then.

When darkness fell, the French trucking company lent to us for only one day vanished. Our DP drivers were willing to continue through the night but Marcel advised Pierre against it for fear they would fall asleep at the wheel.

"Next time, monsieur, I'll have relief drivers trained," said Marcel in the husks of sound he had left for voice. His gentle Flemish face hardened to anger as he glanced over the hundreds still huddled beside the tracks. "If one could have foreseen..."

"You go back, *mon petit.*" Pierre used the "thee" form as with family. "See that your drivers go straight to their rooms with no stopovers in the vodka basements. Report back with them as early as you can get them up in the morning."

We watched Marcel single out his best driver to lead the last convoy. He flagged off the trucks one by one at safe intervals, then climbed into his open jeep to bring up the rear of his nocturnal parade.

"Quel contraste!" said the Belgian nurse. "That boy once was a driver for our royal family. He drove the big black Cadillac of King Leopold."

The French welfare, the Belgian nurse and I decided to remain with Pierre for the night. We drew our two cars together near the tracks, whence for hundreds of yards we could look down a firelit vista of DP's waiting for tomorrow's trucks.

The Poles had gathered up railroad ties strewn about the newly repaired tracks and had stacked these into rectangular frames open at one end where the smoke blew, each side of the burning frame two railroad ties in length. Beyond the fires some were busy building their multiformed luggage into houselike shelters, and between these and the firelight women passed back and forth heating pots of water and stirring together what scraps of food remained to them. A samovar glowed in a circle of shawled shapes that watched it motionlessly. The sandwiches our mess had sent over stuck in our throats.

We walked singly up and down the line listening with our hearts for a sound of pain, complaint or illness. But there was just quiet. Now and again a face lifted to us as if grateful that we had chosen to spend the night with them. The rain had stopped but a bitter damp cold had set in. Once I leaned down to pat the clasped hands of an old lady who peered up at me from under her shawl. *"Sind Sie kalt?"* I asked and she shook her sturdy old head and whispered *"Nein"* with a smile of shy surprise.

That night a permanent picture etched in my memory. It bit sharp and clear the way certain masterpieces engrave themselves as you gaze at them and make them part of you so that you never have to go back for a second look. We had been sleeping fitfully in our cars, three women in one and Pierre in the other. I awoke without reason at four in the morning. There had been no cry, no moan, not even the scrape of a boot heel on gravel to disturb the deathly stillness. I stepped out of the car thinking to warm myself with a walk; then I stood stock-still and stared.

The fires were no longer flaming, but the tough railroad ties had kept their shapes in glowing embers. Four great red quadrangles lay out there along the tracks, and the DP's who had crawled toward these from the outer cold had ranged themselves around them as near as they could get, in a triple row of bodies equidistant from the smoldering ties on all sides. The glowing frames were two man-lengths long and wide and the bodies lay around them in just that way, head to boot or stockinged feet clamped against adjacent wool cap, exactly three deep out from the embers, which was as far as the heat penetrated. Arms were thrown across the faces of those nearest the angular logs and the arms of those in the outside rows, all men, clasped tightly the waists of the middle-lying rows that were made up of women, children and elders. The incandescent ties threw an even red light over these precise diagrams in human geometry and all the rest was total dark.

I walked up and down the line past each one of the red frames to see if in any place the prone bodies paralleling the ties were more than three deep, but there was not a single variation on any side of the smoldering squares, not a spot where two bodies lay, or four. The sleeping forms drawn in toward the heat were laid three deep beside each dying log like some kind of plant or lower animal life demonstrating a tropism.

~ 4 ~

It looked like a toy train chuffing up the long wooded valley from Brückenau. The hills folding in made a funnel that sent its strident whistle ahead of the white plume advancing slowly over the treetops toward the crescent-shaped station of Wildflecken. We listened and watched with astonishment, unable at first to realize that our frenzied days of trucking in humans, potatoes and coal from remote railheads had ended and that an era of easy transport had begun. Army engineers had mended the blasted viaduct near Lohr.

We were so happy looking at our rail connection with the outside world that we ignored the forty cattle cars the little engine shunted into place along our tracks and left there, empty and agape, looking up to us for the next move.

Then over the Signal Corps phone from the remote godhead of division headquarters came a voice informing us that the repatriation program was on. We were expected to produce fifteen hundred willing repatriants for Poland every week until winter closed us in. A military escort was on its way to us to accompany the first transport, scheduled to leave the following day.

"I suppose," said Pierre, "we should consider ourselves honored by having been given one day's advance notice."

But it was easy that first time to produce fifteen hundred repatriants on twenty-four-hour notice. Tak Tak Schön brought down from his committee the repatriation roster that was kept open night and day and we found inscribed enough names of Poles ready and willing to return to the homeland. We merely had to alert these people to be ready for pickup at six next morning.

All through the camp in the chilly dawn, little groups of people sat outside their blockhouses with their piles of luggage, waiting for Marcel's trucks to come along. Neighbors stood around examining with long stares the people who dared to return to the place where their heart was, or a wife, or brothers or parents not seen for more than six years.

Already the repatriants were set apart, not so much by the fact of having made a decision as by the new expression that the act of making a decision had given to their faces, now alight with certainty and no longer able to reflect fear and confusion, even when the stay-behinds deliberately goaded them about Russians waiting to receive them into boxcars labeled for Siberia. For better or for worse, their peaceful faces said, we are going home where we belong. And they sat there with folded hands waiting for the trucks to come.

When the loading started, you would have thought a great train picnic was in the making. The first families delivered to the station began decorating the boxcars, ripping off branches from the plum and apple orchards behind the tracks and nailing the boughs around the door frames, then lacing them with autumn asters the children gathered. Every family had somewhere found lengths of red and white cloth and made the bold two-stripe red and white flag of Poland to nail upright on the corners of the cars. From scraps left over they made rosettes to pin on lapels and caps. Artists begged chalk from Welfare and decorated the sides of the cattle cars with sketches of their heroes and bold slogans in Polish about their never-dying race and the names of villages and hamlets in Poland to which they were bound.

The loading of the special car reserved for the five-day travel ration was a sight that drew the crowds. Our trucks backed up tight against the car door, but through the interstices every item was observed and named aloud — sacks of white-flour bread, cartwheels of Wisconsin cheese, crates of tinned meat and condensed milk. When Tex's warehousemen started counting out the ten-pound tins of jam, you heard a weird approving sound fluttering through the onlookers — *"Mummelid... mummelid!"* — the Polish version of "marmalade."

By eleven, the last of our repatriants had been brought down from camp and we waited for the engine to come. The entire team had come down to see the take-off, to have last visits with cherished workers going home or just to see how their part of the big show was progressing — Welfare counting blankets to make sure everyone had the authorized three, Supply inspecting the candle and firewood distribution to each car, and nurses busy binding the skinned shins and kneecaps of youngsters who were falling all over while Pierre talked officially with the commander of the train escort, a young lieutenant sharp and spotless in well-pressed uniform who was not going to look like that when he delivered his convoy.

I took a last walk through the cattle cars where for five days our Poles would ride, sleep, eat, die and make love and possibly give birth to babies, though we hoped we had weeded out all near-to-term pregnancies. The repatriants had already made themselves at home, twenty-five to a car, including luggage. Their sacks and crates stacked ceiling-high filled all four corners of each car and spilled down around the cleared space by the door where a small wood-burning stove stood in a box of sand, wired to the floor, with its Rube Goldberg chimney elbowing out through a hole in the car wall. Around each stove, folding chairs, cradles and baby buggies were set in cosy confusion, and old ladies, perched high in crannies of the softer luggage, looked down from their safe places like wise old birds on the stampede around the car's opening. Friends and relatives crowded there, taking turns at being hauled up into the car to offer a final *bon voyage* present — a bottle of schnapps, a smoked herring or length of sausage — to give a last letter to be posted inside Poland or a final farewell embrace.

"Dowidzenia... dowidzenia" — Till we meet again. The gentle-sounding syllables were spoken softly under the crying and the laughter like private prayer between friends. They expressed what

every Pole held in his heart, the passionate hope that Poland would really be free as promised.

The first hoot of the oncoming engine sounded up the valley at the same moment that the DP's brass band bore toward us in gathering crescendo, riding down from camp in one of the trucks — a last-minute inspiration of Marcel, who had driven for a king and believed in the regal flourish. Marcel himself was driving the band truck with his pretty Polish interpreter perched beside him all done up in her national costume with bright satin ribbons blowing out from her starched headpiece. The truck moved slowly the length of the platform, stopping beside each boxcar so the band could serenade the departing ones. Concertinas within the cars picked up the wild happy airs of polkas and all the occupants came to the doorways brave and fine in their new UNRRA going-away clothes. They laughed, waved, and where there was a spare inch of space, they clicked their shiny boots together and turned in constricted flings of their native dances.

This was the other side of the coin, a transport viewed from the departure end, but the memories of Gemünden still haunted us and we knew how those gay cars were going to look when they pulled into Dzidiecze, the reception point inside Poland. There would be some illness and misery, maybe even a corpse. The apple boughs would be broken and rain would have washed away the chalked challenges that now so boldly told the world that these were Poles returning in pride and joy to a freed homeland.

Ignatz gave me a hand as I jumped down from the last car. He had brought the Countess down from camp to say farewell to friends in the theater group returning to Warsaw. Her eyes were red from crying.

"*Varsovie... Varsovie,*" she said with a broken sigh of longing. "You must excuse me. It comes back with such pain." She watched the car that had "WARSAW" chalked on its side in block letters enclosed in shaded scrolls. "It almost gives one the illusion the city still exists."

The music had stopped now. Marcel pulled his band truck to the center of the platform as the engine backed in with stench and steam and hooked on. The forty cars clanked with the shock, then the wheels started turning slowly. The band struck up the Polish national anthem.

Pealing brasses, cymbals and rolling drums carried the tremendous theme from end to end of the long train and immediately the repatriants lifted their voices to the hymnlike chant. We stood stiff at salute as the singing cars slid slowly past us, each wide doorway a bower framing groups graded as for family portraits with the smallest in front, each car a burst of song, a flutter of women's kerchiefs, a wild waving of the homemade flags. We stayed at salute until the last choiring car had pulled past. Then we dropped our arms and stood for a long time on the empty platform looking down the track after the green-plumed train trailing smoke and steam and song.

Presently Pierre looked at his team. Some of the women were wiping their eyes.

"*'Allo!*" he cried in a voice none too sure itself. "Here we stand like — how you call it, lumps on lumber?"

"Bumps on logs, Pierre," the Canadian nurse corrected with a thin smile. She was thinking of her eighty-seven babies under six months which the transport had carried away.

"*Bon!* Bumps on logs. We should smile. Be happy. *Sacrebleu!* We now have fifteen hundred less Poles to feed. Such event merits celebration. Tonight after work, you will all come to my house to drink — " he paused to kiss his fingertips — "a Moselle of first quality. I have a cellar. My liaison with the French Zone via those two good-for-nothings." Pierre indicated the two French drivers, who were slightly tipsy from the farewell schnapps drunk with departing Poles. "They go to the British Zone to fetch coal by way of the vineyards," he added proudly.

I thought it would be fine to have a party. It was long overdue. Since we had arrived in Wildflecken one month ago we had hardly had time to make the acquaintance of the UNRRA people who were holding down the camp when we came. We broke bread together daily but at differing hours and we still tended toward national grouping at the mess table, the Dutch at their end, the

Belgians as far from these as they could get, the French in their garrulous huddles and the English-speaking drifting everywhere except together. Plenty of small adjustments would have to be made, I reflected, before the winter snows would seal us off from the outside world for four long months.

Our billets tended to separate us yet another way. We lived in a row of stucco houses, formerly German officers' quarters, with certain houses reserved for women, certain ones for men, while Pierre inhabited the big verandaed white house of the former camp *Kommandant,* which sat up the hill from our graveled "UNRRA Street." We had a clubroom arranged by the welfare girls but usually when we came down from camp we were too tired to cross the road to it. What scraps of personal life we still retained were shared with the occupants of the house we inhabited.

But we were not destined to have a party that night after our first transport out to Poland. Not until the fifteen-foot drifts of snow, which had made impossible any movement in or out of camp, had melted were we to get together at last as a team united for pleasure purposes only. And then we would be lifting our glasses to toast many new faces and the few who remained of our original team, as survivors.

At sundown of that same day another string of boxcars stood in our railroad station, not empty and agape this time, but crammed with incoming refugees who had already built fires along the cobbled platform when we descended the hill for dinner.

This was the prelude to a prolonged and frantic activity that began to seem like a horrible parody of the game put-'n'-take. During the next sixty days more than ten thousand DP's came in or went out from our camp. Army put DP's in and we shipped them out, as many as were willing to go home. The in-transports were all like the first one except that they came practically to our doorstep now and their human cargoes grew more pitiable as the cold increased. The out-transports were repetitions of our first repatriation train except that now we accomplished our loadings like a reflex action requiring no thought.

It seemed that the roarings up and down our cobbled hill of the worn trucks loaded high with humans never ceased. We became like slaves to that curve of railroad track beneath our windows and we learned to dread our first look toward it when we raised our billet blinds each morning, for fear we would see, as we usually did, another string of boxcars waiting for us in the freezing dawn with thin streamers of smoke issuing from some of the car chimneys but not from all, since not all Poles could discipline themselves to ration their wood allotment for the journey. Those who burned it all joyously on the first day or so shivered the rest of the way and arrived with pneumonia.

We would stare across the space separating bedrooms from railroad tracks at the closed sliding doors of the smokeless cars, and even as we were hastily pulling on clothes, we would be seeing and smelling those fetid interiors and feeling on our cold cheeks the brush of the warmth that would flow from them when we shoved back the doors to unload.

Time folded up like the closed concertinas our refugees now carried mutely with no will to extend in song the bitterness of any single moment. The burning beauty of our Bavarian hills clothed in scarlet and gold told us that autumn was passing. Once Ignatz brought a great bunch of autumn crocus, so I knew that was what made the saffron carpet in the meadows behind the station. When the crocus were gone, he brought a basket of fist-sized *Steinpilze,* the famous mushroom of Bavaria.

Then one night a howling north wind blew down our valley and took every bright leaf from the trees. Freezing rain fell and we all turned into troglodytes in our hooded raincoats and clumping galoshes. We prayed for the imminent snows to shut us off from the world of transports and to spare us the military inspections which harassed us after Patton lost command of the Third Army and General Truscott took over. The "new broom" officers came through camp and made suggestions that kept us crazy for weeks at a time, undoing past work, redoing it the new way and revamping all reports to fit the orders in the sheaves of directives which we had to study at night because we still had fifteen thousand people to take care of during the days.

Now and again in the grueling stretch before the first salvational snows, a team member reached the limit of his endurance and decamped. The first to go was our pair of French drivers. They were simple good men who never in their lives had stolen a nut or a bolt, but one night they took a truck and drove out the main gate and kept going until they reached Paris, their wives, and the dear normalcy of their beloved boulevards. Two Dutch went next, thumbing a ride in an Army truck that was going their way. Some team members asked for transfers to outfits that were stationed in cities where Army was already beginning to set up officers' clubs and movie houses.

Replacements brought in new blood and new languages. A Cuban doctor and a Venezuelan doctor and a Swedish supply man added their tongues to our international babel, and the special clipped accent of New Zealand was contributed by a woman named Londa, who arrived with one of the incoming transports, looking like a DP herself after the two-day ride up from Munich in a boxcar. She was a lively and attractive woman in her mid-thirties, full of violent opinions on the way the DP operation was being handled, fighting the cause of the DP as if it were her own.

"There are some madmen sitting up topside," she told us. Her black eyes seemed to explode. "Do you know what they're talking about down Munich way? Forced repatriation!"

Londa had been assigned for a time to a southern camp when its Russian refugees, mainly prisoners of war, had been sent back to Russia under terms of the Yalta Agreement. She told us how the Russian PW's had slashed their wrists, stripped naked and hanged themselves rather than get into the repatriation train. Even after every destructive object was taken from them they still found ways to suicide. She could never understand how Stalin had sold his idea to Roosevelt and Churchill that there had been no Russian prisoners of war taken by the Germans, only deserters.

"After that show, some people are talking of forced repatriation for our United Nations DP's, if you can imagine such insanity."

We could not believe it, but on the other hand we were hundreds of miles from where policy was being made. The UNRRA and Army directives that filtered down to us often made us wonder if anyone around those top-level round tables had ever seen a DP. Our repatriation statistics sent weekly to H.Q. were regarded as a sort of scoreboard to be compared with the records of other repatriating camps. The outfits that fell behind were accused of antirepatriation sentiments.

Ignatz gazed respectfully at the map of the new Poland which had been sent to encourage the homebound movements. He told me why, since we had placarded the camp bulletin boards with it, our repatriation had dropped off.

He ran his finger down the eastern frontier, following the River Bug that marked it. He brushed his fingers over the land east of Warsaw, trailed them down through Lember and Odessa on the Black Sea, the territory ceded to Russia by a treaty signed in Moscow just one month before; then he hunted until he found a small village a few kilometers inland on the Russian side of the Bug.

"Heimat," he said softly. "My homeland."

"But you wouldn't be forced to cross the Bug if you repatriated," I said. "Just look what Poland got in exchange." I showed him the thousands of square miles enclosed in Poland's new western addition, the former German provinces of Silesia, Pomerania and West Prussia, rich in coal and industry. I asked the Countess to tell him in Polish that with his mechanical genius he could walk into that new territory and set himself up in business immediately. The two of them talked back and forth with a curious old smile on their faces as if they were humoring me. Then Ignatz bowed and put his finger again on the small village inside the USSR.

"They would return him there," said the Countess. "No matter where inside Poland UNRRA would set him down. Homeland is homeland, he says, and when that village name would be seen on his papers, that is where he would be sent. He begs your pardon for disagreeing with you, but he would never set foot on Polish soil as long as his natal village is on the Russian side of the new line."

The Poles clustered around the bulletin boards looking at the map of new Poland. You could tell from their faces which ones came from east of the River Bug. Some of the women wept quietly while the men stared in a disbelief too keen for comment, uttering only the names of home towns in a lost litany of sorrowful sounds... "Lwow... Rovno... Stanislav..."

I studied a German atlas found in my billet and learned that before World War II, Poland had had an area of some one hundred and fifty thousand square miles, and that the territory east of the Bug which we had ceded to Russia comprised nearly seventy thousand square miles. I tried to imagine how I would feel were I shown a map of the United States with almost half its territory ceded to a foreign power — for example, everything from the Missouri River to the Pacific Coast, with about thirty-eight thousand square miles of Canada tossed in as recompense, as Silesia, Pomerania and West Prussia had been given to Poland. I gave my California childhood to one of those Poles from east of the Bug and then I tried out my paraphrased sales talk on repatriation. "Now look at this fine industrial area up around Quebec, or at these forest lands farther north. You can resettle there and build a new life so that eventually you'll forget all about San Francisco over there on the other side of the new frontier..."

That's as far as I got. I looked at San Francisco closed forever to me by an imaginary iron curtain and I saw our repatriation job for the first time in its true perspective, one half of it a reasonable solution, the other half something like this:

"Be a pioneer in Pomerania! UNRRA will give you a cow and a plow. Your Polish Provisional Government will give you farm acreage, fine fat German acres with a few of the Germans still hanging around. However, those dispossessed supermen are soon to be removed so you won't be troubled by their present raids on the struggling new farms. Even the towns will lose their German names. Look, you've already changed Breslau to Wroclaw. It's

Poland already. Get in on the ground floor. Free cow. Free plow. Sacks of seed too, all free."

Fortunately, we still had enough Poles from the regions around the great old cities of Warsaw, Cracow and Lublin to keep our repatriation register busy and our transports reasonably filled. So we did not have to begin just then to urge the debatable joys of pioneering in an alien annexation. That would come in the spring, unless something happened meanwhile. There was a straw in the wind...

I knew he was a Russian the instant he entered my office. I knew by the way the Countess stiffened, though nothing that I could see indicated his origin. He had the most alert and passionate face I had ever gazed upon, as if the dance music of Borodin had materialized in the flesh. He stood a little less tall than I, so I was looking directly at his extraordinary pelt of hair, exactly like clipped beaver fur. His sunken eyes were full of motion and light, and when he began telling his story in Russian to the Countess, he gestured with ballet movements.

His name was Piotr. He was a Russian prisoner of war who had spent three years in German prison pens. The Amerikanskis released him when they came through and, according to some agreement which he never believed the Allies had made, they turned him over to the Russians, who transported him to another pen just inside the frontier of Russia. There he heard about Stalin's pronouncement that there had been no Russian prisoners of war, only deserters. In regular convoys groups from this prison pen were sent "home," but they never arrived because their families came to the outside of the barbed wire and asked where they were. They were never heard from again. Occasionally a few tried the escape route back into Occupied Germany and finally Piotr tried it also.

His ballet presentation grew more precise as he described a week of walking until he had passed the Zone lines separating Russian-occupied from American-occupied Germany. Daytimes he slept in hideouts. He carried no food, but nights, when he walked, he felt around in the dark for the feathery foliage of carrots which told him where to dig when crossing truck farms. Toward the fifth day he began to get lightheaded. I thought he was going right off into a toe dance when he described how it was walking in the dark and hearing voices and seeing lights where none were. Finally, one night when he judged he must be well inside the American Zone of Occupation, he tapped at the door of a German farm and asked for food in the broken German he had picked up in their prison pens. The Germans gave him food and also clothes to cover his Russian uniform. They gave road directions. Thus from farm to farm he progressed toward the west. At last he came to our piney mountains and circled for two days around the camp wondering if he dared come in and ask for food. He heard Poles talking as they went in and out through the woods and gathered that the camp was not a prison place but some sort of free city run by kind foreigners from overseas. On one of his night prowls he encountered a Pole who had been in the same prison pen with him. His Polish friend brought him into the camp and directly to our office door. Piotr said he had heard that somewhere in the American Zone there was a camp for Russian PW's where honorable ex-soldiers were permitted to remain until Stalin promised not to punish them. We had heard this rumor also but to our knowledge it was only a forlorn dream.

When she finished translating, the Countess did not ask me what to do. She called the Polish committee president and asked him to come at once to see something special. Tak Tak Schön came promptly. Piotr stood at attention before him and recited his whole story all over again, and showed papers documenting the truth of all he related. Then, although I knew no Russian, I understood that Piotr had asked asylum in our camp. A hunted look came into his eyes. The eyes clung to Tak Tak's face and the great fleece coat that had been so full of movement hung dead-quiet as if breathing beneath it had stopped.

"He could be absorbed as a Pole," said the Countess quietly. "Think of all the Ukrainians we have here, registered as Poles. Could you send a creature like that back to certain death?"

Tak Tak could not, of course. He lifted a corner of the German shepherd fleece coat and looked at the nails and wire holding up out of sight the skirt of the Russian greatcoat. He examined Piotr's boots, pointed-toed like Polish boots but with the heels set in at a different angle.

"Tell him I can issue a pair of shoes," I said.

"I'll keep him with me for a day or so," Tak Tak said finally. "When the next transport comes in, we'll register him in regularly like any other newcomer."

The next transport came that evening. I never saw Piotr again though often I looked among our multitudes for his face. Later the Countess reported that he had been safely sequestered in our statistics.

~ 5 ~

No respectable dictionary contains the word "winterization," but Army directives were full of it now, including its verb "winterize," to make ready for winter. The winterization program was another scoreboard, like the repatriation program, to which we reported weekly how many tons of potatoes had been hauled in and stored, how many cubic feet of wood had been chopped, and what was our progress on procuring the thirty-day winter reserve of food which Army would allow us to keep on hand in our warehouses — if we could get through their red tape and wrench it from their supply depots.

The food problem was beginning to frighten us. With the exception of imported staples such as sugar, coffee, oils and condiments, we took our DP food from German sources by order of Military Government. Our supply men went forth daily to fight with German mayors who were supposed to secure from local farmers the required amounts of fresh meat, milk, cereals, potatoes and vegetables. As summer crops dried up our men's faces seemed to shrink. The six hundred tons of food our DP's ate up each month had to be fought for literally ton by ton. Everyone on the team except doctors and nurses was involved in this struggle, lending a hand to our overworked Supply in the vast warehouse area at the summit of our camp.

Meanwhile delegations from the camp queued up outside our headquarters with samples of some of the food that comprised the daily two thousand calories. Pierre and I were continually peering into small pots containing the portion of soup doled out for a midday meal with one marble-sized meatball allowed to each inhabitant, or into samples of milk from the children's kitchen containing a queer floating substance which the DP's called "silver fish," claiming it a form of German sabotage. Continuously too we were answering phone calls from our local Military Government complaining about the increasing disappearances from German farms of cows and hogs which were assumed to have been smuggled into camp by our "marauding DP's."

Then Army decided to encourage repatriation by giving a fourteen-day food ration to each repatriant, which reduced our painfully acquired hoard of the winter food reserve. We were assured that we would get this food back from Army since the winter reserve was holy and untouchable except in time of disaster. All we had to do was put in a requisition. That was the same as saying, All you have to do is shoot an arrow into the air.

For more than two months with no result we had been requisitioning stoves and stovepipe to complete the winterization of the twenty-eight hundred rooms in our sixty blockhouses. The sole requisition on which we received reply was one for two thousand rubber glove-fingers needed by our doctors for the VD examination which Army ordered made on all women in the camp. We received exactly six glove-fingers from the Medical Supply dump and against the remainder of our two-thousand request was the familiar red stamp "Not available." Somehow, with those six glove-fingers, our doctors managed to examine our five thousand women over the age of sixteen.

The night our Venezuelan doctor came to the mess and told Pierre that he could report that the VD examinations were completed in our camp, Londa flew at him like a harpy. He listened to her tirade with a gentle smile as he meticulously cut away the fat from his meat because he was developing ulcers.

"I don't know why you even attempted it," Londa raged. "I'd like to have seen the Army medics handed a job like that. Six glove-fingers for five thousand women. You know what those medics would have told their CO to do with those glove-fingers?

Do you know, Pedro?" She thrust her half-finished plate aside. "Really, what we're expected to do with no help from anywhere, from anyone..."

"Don't strike him," I said; "he was just doing the impossible. Haven't you heard, Londa? That's what we're famous for."

"Famous!" The New Zealander rose abruptly from the table, her dessert fruit in her hand. She pointed to all the empty places, those of the supply men still out after dark fighting to get tomorrow's milk for our children, of the nurses still up in camp trying to locate and isolate the measles cases the last transport had introduced, and at the vacant chair of our Belgian engineer, who was exploring the freezing warehouses in hopes of uncovering in the masses of German matériel the hundreds of light sockets and switches he still needed to complete his winterization of the DP living quarters.

"Do you know what *I* think?" Londa swung around with her hand on the doorknob, looking as if she were going to tear it off and throw it at us to try to knock some sense into us. "I think we've all gone crazy. Just plain old-fashioned crazy, the whole Godforsaken pack of us."

She flung open the door and a redheaded sergeant standing in the doorway said, "You do, do you?" He swept her with a look of admiration — she was always beautiful in anger.

"Well, lady, wait till you see what *I've* brought. Then you'll really know what it is to be nuts."

The sergeant walked over to Pierre at the head of the table. He thumped down in front of him the large box he was carrying.

"You're in command here, I take it." The sergeant clapped a sheaf of directives down on top of the box.

"This is an American Red Cross PW food parcel. And this here is General Eisenhower's poop on how it's to be broken down."

We slit the gummed tape sealing the carton. We had no idea what the sergeant was talking about until we got the box open. Our eyes popped as we lifted out a pound package of cube sugar, tins of Cheddar cheese, of sardines, Nescafé, corned beef, tuna, Spam, dried milk, Crisco, a half-pound chocolate bar and seven packs of American cigarettes.

"That's to help out the DP food ration," said the sergeant. "Your troubles are over for winter food. There's about fourteen thousand calories in that box. You get one per month per DP. I've got four boxcars of this stuff down on the tracks, fifteen thousand food parcels. Got orders to stick around with my guard until you've unloaded. Then it's your baby."

Londa brought him coffee, her nerves forgotten in the excitement. We all talked at once. We looked again at each item of the Red Cross prisoner-of-war food parcel. The Europeans had not seen such luxury foods since 1939 and some had never seen Nescafé, Spam and vitamin tablets. Since Pearl Harbor, I had not seen all those things we "gave up" for three years or more. I looked at the tuna that had been practically unprocurable for my war-worker lunches. I read the familiar names of Camel, Lucky Strike, Chesterfield, and thought of the war-baby cigarettes for which we had queued up in the shipyards.

"You say one food parcel per month for *every* DP in Germany?" I asked.

"Yep," said the sergeant, blowing on his coffee.

"For how long?" asked Londa.

"Jeez... if you could see them Army depots, you'd say for years."

"We must have thought a lot of our boys would be behind barbed wire," I said. It seemed a strange twist of fate that those superb high-calorie foods that had disappeared from our chain-store shelves for all those years should now turn up with such a different destiny.

"Gott sei dank, as we say over here," said the sergeant with a freckled grin, "it ain't us that's gonna eat 'em."

Pierre was scribbling on his paper napkin. He looked a bit wild when he laid down his pencil.

"I make it that with fifteen thousand parcels, seven packs of cigarettes in each, we have a hundred and five thousand packages of cigarettes," he said unbelievingly.

"That's just what I mean, chief," said the sergeant. "Roughly ten thousand cartons — a thousand reichsmarks the carton in the black market. You got about ten million reichsmarks right there to take care of, not to mention what Crisco, Nescafé and chocolate brings. It ain't hay what I've got sittin' down there on the tracks. Crazy, see what I mean?" He turned to Londa. "Lady, you ain't seen nuthin' yet!"

We began to see something even before we got the boxcars unloaded, but not the black market lust the sergeant had warned us about. That would come later, much later. First we were to see the more basic reaction of hungry people who had lived for more than six years on black bread and potato soup and who now had a mountain of delectable foreign foods unloaded in their midst. We were so stunned thinking of the value of the cigarettes which we would have to guard with questionable DP police, it did not occur to us that one taste of a fatty pink slice of Spam, for example, would be enough to throw our camp into a maddened uproar.

We started unloading next morning as soon as the Polish committee had selected a group of "men of confidence" to pass the parcels from boxcar to trucks. Marcel delegated his most trustworthy drivers to the long haul from station to Central Supply, uphill through pine woods all the way in slow second gear. DP police were stationed at intervals to see that no packages were tossed off en route and team members took up posts where they could watch the DP police.

But it was as if the whole population of Poles had smelled that food, right through the heavy cartons that packaged it, right through the tin that sealed in each wondrous unheard-of item. Before the first trucks had discharged their loads in the warehouse (which our engineer was hastily fitting up with iron window bars) the woods bordering the main road were alive with scurrying forms. Camp streets thronged with DP's chattering a language that did not even sound like Polish. Actually, it was the language of hysteria.

Londa worked in the warehouse supervising the "men of confidence" who were unloading and stacking the boxes. I told her my suspicions.

"It's not possible," she said. "They haven't made off with a single parcel yet. Every truck has tallied correctly with what it left the station with." She was transformed by happiness. She talked about what the windfall of vitamins would do for her rickety DP children. She planned a special kitchen where the children could have hot chocolate every afternoon. "A supplemental feeding," she rejoiced. "What I've been fighting for ever since I came here."

A great block of food parcels was already stacked fifteen boxes high with the build-on end tapering down from the top like stairs. The Poles ran up and down this stairway of food with a joyous agility seldom seen in their motions of work. They too were transformed with expectations.

When Ignatz drove me back to the station the excitement had lifted another octave. A noisy crowd cheered my UNRRA car and shouted *"Pakiety... pakiety!"* — the package.

"Wunderbar," said Ignatz, *"diese Schinken!"* We were learning German together. We spoke it like children, without verbs. But I knew the noun for ham.

"What ham?" I asked.

"This ham in the pretty boxes." Spam! I knew it.

"Ignatz... already?" I gestured down the throat, then at the crowds.

"Na-tür-lich!" Ignatz drew out the word "naturally" to shame me for my slow wit.

"How?"

He took one hand from the wheel and made small back-sweeping gestures. *"Comme ci, comme ça,"* he laughed, echoing Pierre's frequent phrase.

When I got to the station I found Pierre talking with the sergeant.

"Listen," I said, "the camp's on its ear. They've already eaten some of this stuff. They *know* what's in the boxes."

"Impossible, my little *fleur bleue*," Pierre said with composure. "I've been right here watching all. The sergeant's men move from car to car with the workers." His fond regard suggested to the onlooker that our relationship had sprung from mutual interest in things far more delicate than strings of boxcars and windy warehouses and I wished that the sergeant knew that "blue flower" was only the French for "greenhorn."

"Ignatz said..."

"You and your dear Ignatz! You know" — Pierre turned to the sergeant — "this woman of the world is a little blue flower, she believes everything her driver tells her."

"Well," said the sergeant, "as a matter of fact, she's right. Some of the DP's came snoopin' around the cars last night. We made 'em chop our firewood. So we gave them some of the cans from boxes that had busted open..."

He misread the look on Pierre's face.

"We got an overage for breakage en route," he added quickly.

By the time we reached our office, several hundred DP's were congregated outside headquarters. They hailed Pierre as if he were Santa Claus and gave three brisk vivas for the *"Pakiety... pakiety... pakiety."* They were positive that the packages were going to be handed out whole. One for each DP per month had already flashed over their grapevine.

The Countess translated into Polish, German and Russian the precise directions on how the boxes were to be broken down, the foods stored on warehouse shelves and, as needed, distributed to the kitchens to supplement the regular ration. We were also ordered to burn the empty cartons to prevent the Red Cross symbol from being used again, for purposes other than merciful, such as sale to the Germans, filled with less nourishing contents. We did not translate that part for fear it would give our Poles more ideas than they already had. We thanked God that Eisenhower had signed the directive. No name in Germany carried more weight. Our Poles had already made new signs for the camp's main square originally called Adolf-Hitlerplatz; they renamed it Eisenhowerplatz. We typed Eisenhower's name large at the bottom of our translation and surrounded it with bands of typewriter stars.

We called Tak Tak Schön for a conference with the police chief and the scout leader. We knew by then that none of our Spam-maddened adults could be trusted with the opening of the food parcels. I had convinced Pierre that Londa and I could organize the scouts for this work. I asked for fifty to be sent to the warehouse early next morning, boys and girls but none under fourteen.

That night while our Poles were reading on bulletin boards the death of their *pakiety* hopes, Londa and I worked in the warehouse setting up a production line. The dimension of the job ahead staggered us. The heavy cardboard flaps of the Red Cross boxes were glued as well as gum-taped, requiring an ax to pry them open. Each box contained twenty-five separate items.

Every time I looked at the stacked boxes looming like ancient step pyramids in the warehouse gloom, I could feel trouble brewing. I tried to calculate how long it would be before we could get that food started on its way to the kitchens to assuage the awakened hunger of those who had already tasted it and the fiercely tantalized imaginations of those who had only heard how it tasted.

"It's fantastic," said Londa. "Food like this in the middle of starving Europe." She read a label on a sardine tin. "Packed in pure olive oil — Rockland, Maine."

"Listen, I've been figuring. Do you realize that in those mountains of boxes there are exactly three hundred and seventy-five thousand individual items that will have to be handled one by one?"

"Dear God, no!" Londa dropped the tins she was carrying and stared at the angular stacks.

"It will take forever, with children," she said.

"Maybe not. Maybe they'll do it like a game. You know," I said, "sort of like playing store." I was ashamed of the phrase as soon as I said it. Playing store — a memory from an unmolested childhood. "We'll use those box stalls for food bins."

We put samples of each food in a separate stall so our scouts would know where things should go. The light bulb swaying in the warehouse draft threw our shadows over the long table we had set up, low enough for a child to work at. When we stooped over it, it looked like furniture for infants.

Next morning Wildflecken was a city in revolt. Our DP workers staged a sit-down strike. Eight hundred woodcutters who went daily to the woods refused to get into the waiting trucks. The garbage disposal squad sent their trucks back empty to the motor pool. The carpenters and bricklayers detailed to blockhouse repair failed to report to the engineering chief.

The Poles intended to have a Red Cross parcel handed out to them whole. No monkey business about distribution through the thieving chefs of their camp kitchens, no tomfoolery about making one box last a whole month when it could be enjoyed in a single night of magnificent celebration.

"Pakiety... pakiety." The whole camp resounded to the one-word chant that picked up volume and insistence each time an UNRRA car threaded the striking crowds. There would have been something comical in the demonstration if you had not thought of the years of privation that lay behind it, the years of longing for a taste of the good things of life. *"Pakiety,"* they called like thwarted children. Oh please just once, their faces said, let us gorge our fill on liver paste, chocolate and juicy pink salmon; let us each know the feel in our pockets of seven whole packs of American cigarettes, just once, for the first time in our lives.

Londa and I waited for the scouts at the barred gate to Central Supply. We heard them coming before we saw them. Their scout songs rang through the woods as if they were off on some wondrous jamboree. Then we saw them marching up the hill toward us, fifty little boys and girls two abreast and in close formation, swinging their arms and singing lustily. A crowd of strikers congregated outside the gate to prevent any workers from opening the Red Cross parcels, stepped back and made a clear path for the singing scouts. It had not yet occurred to the strikers that we were going to start the job with the only group we dared to trust.

Once inside the cavernous warehouse, we lined up the scouts beside the long table that held twenty-five food items spaced at intervals on both sides. The Countess talked in a storytelling voice as she went from tin, to carton, to envelope, briefly lifting each and telling what it was and how there were fourteen thousand, nine hundred and ninety-nine others exactly like it which had to be sorted out and put in those separate stalls at the rear where horses used to be.

When the chewing gum, the chocolate and the tins of jam were held up before those fifty pairs of child eyes, I thought for one wild moment that I was going to sob. The wide blue eyes regarded unwaveringly, as in a trance, a raspberry jam label depicting a solid mass of red berries dripping with sugary highlights, a packaged bar wrapped in chocolate-colored paper scored off in small squares like the chocolate inside, three sticks of gum which until then had been thought of as something that came only from the person of the American soldier. You knew that these things must have torn at the vitals of those children though not one of them gave any outward sign. They stood stiffly with arms at their sides looking up at the Countess with faces of wonder.

It was better when the children began handling the foods. The unbearable wonderstruck expressions left their faces as their fingers got used to the feel of the tins. Each child accustomed himself to the appearance and shape of the one item for which he was responsible. Ignatz tore open the tough box flaps and shoved the full boxes down the production-line table while the little hands reached in from both sides. The scouts worked with furious concentration, not at all like shopkeepers. At first they did not talk, as if in school; but after the first hour they were calling back and forth to each other in muffled voices, saying things that made the whole table titter.

"They've named each other after the product they sort," said the Countess. "Mr. Tuna has just remarked to Mr. Salmon that his face was pink. Mr. Sugar says to Miss Tea Bags that they ought to get along together despite the difference in their ages." She wiped her eyes and pointed to the pigtailed girl at the end of the table who collected the small envelopes of vitamins from each parcel. "They call her Miss Pill; they think those vitamins are medicine."

Mr. Milk Powder, handling the largest tins, was the first to fill a carton with his product. He called for a grownup to lift it away to the stalls, where other scouts crouched at the task of stacking the separated items. Within the first hour the children had swung into their jobs like some piece of intricately co-ordinated machinery and the pile of emptied cartons grew high enough to start the burning.

I walked back and forth, bending, shoving, lifting, lending a hand wherever needed, and watching the children all the time. I found myself studying their quick precise gestures as if I had been drawn into some child world of strange intensity whose meaning eluded me. Through the high cobwebbed windows the morning sun penetrated as a diffused moonlight which fell on the absorbed children and made them seem more like memories of children recalled across gray spaces of time.

When I carried filled boxes over to the storage stalls, I stared at the children crouching there, stacking their individual products in automatic patterns of neatness and efficiency. A small girl in charge of the tapered tins of corned beef deftly alternated them to make a solid stack that would not spill sideways. The sardine boy stacked his oval tins in one corner of his stall and his square tins in another corner. Even the littlest ones knew what to do without asking questions.

I stood beside the lad in charge of cigarettes at the end of the unpacking table, watching how he patted the packs in edgewise until he came to the top of the box. I waited for the next cigarettes to come down the table to see what he would do. He took the next seven packages and laid them in flat for the final layer, bringing it exactly flush with the top of the box.

"Schön!" I said, admiring his ingenuity.

He looked up and grinned with professional pride. The one tooth missing in front gave his face the classical look of the rugged small boy the world over.

"Wie in der Fabrik," he said, patting his perfect packing with one stubby hand.

As in the factory! For an instant I did not take it in. It was as if Huckleberry Finn had spoken out of character. He brushed back a shock of sunbleached hair and held up his fingers fanned out to five.

"Fünf Jahre," he said, nodding like an old man.

That was the answer that had eluded me. That was the explanation for the children's dexterity and knowingness with small objects. The Germans had used their fast fingers in factories and war plants, had trained them to handle small parts with speed and precision. The Countess confirmed my sickening guess.

"Probably most of these over fifteen," she said, "had five years of slave labor in the factories before liberation. They took them as early as ten years, especially when they were bright and clever."

"I'm going to take them off this job," I said in fury.

"Oh, but you cannot," said the Countess. "You must believe me, they are happy here. If you could only understand what they are saying to each other. This is something new and exciting to do. Their pride of the scout... if you dismissed them now, they would feel they had failed you."

"Dismiss?" cried Londa coming up with her tally sheet. "Who's talking of dismissing them? Look here. They've already opened over seven hundred parcels. More than seventeen thousand tins are already sorted and shelved. It's unbelievable."

"It *will* be when I tell you why," I said. I knew what happened to her welfare heart when I told her. "In any event," I added, "you weren't so damned naïve as to say it would be like playing store. Dear God, when will I ever learn what I'm up against?"

When the noon siren sounded we lined up the children and gave to each a large piece of vitaminized chocolate from broken bars. We told them that a new scout crew was coming for the afternoon shift. Their faces refused to believe this, they pled to be allowed to come too. We swung open the big warehouse door saying no, no, to their begging faces. Then we saw the greatly enlarged crowd of demonstrators waiting outside the barred gate of Central Supply.

Something within me burst wide open with fury. I had never before felt anything but loving compassion for the DP. No matter what he did, I had always been able to find a reason to justify him. With something like shock I felt the adrenalin shooting into my blood stream. I left Londa with the scouts and went forward with the Countess toward the gate.

I felt like somebody else walking in wrath toward the murmuring crowd. In that transformed moment, I hated the displaced person and every cause behind him that had made him what he was. I despised the insanity of international relief that imagined something could be done with this ruin in the human soul, so much more fearful than all the mountains of rubble strewn over the face of Europe. I climbed to the top of the guardhouse steps and pulled the Countess up beside me.

"Tell those bastards to listen to me," I said. She gave me a shocked look. *"Salauds* — that's what I said."

"Pani Direktor..." Her strong clear voice reached to the edge of the crowd. I saw some familiar faces — a man for whom I had interceded with Military Government, a woman to whom I had given a pass for reasons not in the rules. I stared at these with special loathing. The Countess ceased speaking.

Slowly, in a voice that did not sound like mine, I spoke to the gaping crowd, pausing long between phrases and watching the Countess with white-hot anger ready for her too if I could detect her softening a single syllable. I called them a pack of jealous lazy bums, a disgrace to the name of the displaced person whose cause the UNRRA was trying to sell to a world that was not interested. And who would want people like you? I cried. I told them of the great work their sons and daughters had just accomplished, a job to put them all to shame if they had any shame left in them. When I spoke of the scouts, my voice cracked. I shook my fist and finished with threats.

If any man or woman so much as lifted a finger to one of my scouts, or even taunted him with a word, I would throw that person into the American jail in Brückenau and personally see to it that he sat there for a year. Then I stepped down and told the guard to open the gate.

Ignatz brought up my car. I pushed him over to the passenger place and took the wheel. I was ready to run down any Pole who refused to clear a path for the oncoming scouts. I waited until their singing column was right behind my car, then I drove into the crowd in low gear. The demonstrators stepped back swiftly.

In the rear-view mirror I could see the column of towheads following the car like a long blond tail with plenty of room to swing in. I drove slowly until we came to one of the camp streets where ordinary traffic circulated. Then I stopped the car and took Londa in.

"Good show, old thing," Londa said crisply. She knew that I was ready to burst into tears.

"All in a day's work, I guess..." The shameful anger was gone. My only feeling was one of dull humiliation. "Screaming at them like a virago," I said. "Threatening those poor devils with jail." The DP's prompt obedience to anger and threats seemed almost the worst discovery I had yet made about them.

Pierre was doing it differently at the headquarters. His crowd was bigger than the one I had tackled. He had translating for him a former member of the Polish parliament who spoke French in fluent idiom. Pierre said he didn't give a damn if the Poles never went back to the woods. It wasn't *his* behind that would freeze in winter when there was no more firewood to distribute. The Poles had clamored for self-government through their committee and had been given it. If this was the way they wanted to run their affairs, it would be unpardonable for him to step in and change things. Very possibly the Poles liked the smell of uncollected garbage in their blockhouses... *Chacun à son goût,* each to his taste. And was it not droll that their bakers thought UNRRA would weep in anxiety for the bakery strike? UNRRA got its bread from the Army commissary. Only the self-governing people of the camp would be tightening their belts. *Bref, mes enfants,* you have made your bed.

"Je m'en fiche!" Pierre's final shrug had the magnitude of a *monument historique.*

The Poles shifted from foot to foot while trying to look tough and full of menace. You knew that they were going back to work. But not immediately. They could not afford to lose face too quickly.

Pierre strode through the crowd, glaring like an annoyed householder at the trampled grass and broken bushes fronting the headquarters building. When he climbed into my waiting car, I saw he was shaking like a leaf.

~ 6 ~

Nearly every kind of life gives a respite of some sort, a time to sit back and take stock, to find out where you are going and why. But our life with the DP's in that first postwar winter gave no such pause. We were engaged in a race against time to get everything essential stored in our warehouses before the first snows. And we were working with human beings, who never remain the same for any consecutive period but go up and down the scale, evolving or disintegrating, depending on the stamina of the individual concerned. Each time one of us attempted a conclusive statement on the displaced person, some immediate new development upset the conclusion.

A new doctor joined the team, a thin nervous Medical captain who would never sit down at table for breakfast but would walk back and forth with his cup of coffee in one hand and pellets of bicarbonate in the other, discussing the DP's as if they were a species he had examined under the microscope and knew with exactitude. "They are all professional DP's by now... we've welfared them into a permanent state of the gimmes," he would say.

The first time I heard "professional DP's" the phrase shocked me. The doctor knew this and would repeat "Gimme, gimme" in German, Russian and Polish, walking around the breakfast table with his hand outstretched like a DP. I argued back in heat and always lost. I did not speak the language of the DP's as he did, the doctor would say, so how could I know what they were thinking?

It was Ignatz who eventually gave the lie to the doctor's easy generality about DP's being all professional. In the last lap of the winterization race, Ignatz was with me like a shadow. The vast uproar over the Red Cross parcels subsided after the first distribution of those foodstuffs through the camp kitchens as a supplement to the daily ration — one tin of tuna to each on a day when the German butchers had given us meat containing more than the twenty-five per cent bone which Military Government permitted. The Poles stood in their dry-ration breadlines watching their chefs count out the round tins, laying many on the long loaves destined for large families or a single tin on the thick slice for the bachelor, and their eyes were like gun barrels geared to a target. Tense yet tranquil, they knew another day would come when the Germans would foist off on us a meat that was mostly bone... then that strange *Schinken* called Spam would have its turn.

Meanwhile, huge convoys of winter clothing were coming into camp. Presently the attention of the Poles shifted from Spam to winter overcoats — which seemed to prove the doctor's point.

Ignatz kept vigil for the clothing convoys as if he were an UNRRA officer. At all hours the calls came through from the main gate — "Clothing convoy going through to warehouse." Those of us not bedridden with colds, flu or plain exhaustion would jump into our clothes, rouse our drivers, who now lived in UNRRA Street, and hurry up to the windy warehouse to stand by and tally in while the trucks unloaded enormous sacks of coats and dresses, old and new, of trousers, shirts and shoes, shoes, shoes.

Filthy in fatigues, bearded, brutalized by the long hauls in freezing winter rains, the GI's driving the trucks were unrecognizable as Americans. They too were caught in the killing momentum of winterization. They snored over their wheels until the last sack was rolled from their trucks. Then they abruptly awoke, snatched our signed receipt and roared away into the dark not even pausing for the coffee we made for them in the mess. The tons of clothing they left with us had to be sorted and inventoried before distribution, another colossal drudgery with deadline set.

Directives said that two weeks after reception, the clothing was supposed to be on the back of the DP.

The day when Ignatz inadvertently produced the argument with which I could blast the word "professional" forever from the doctor's speech began like any other in the past weeks — a shivering dawn after a zero night, Ignatz out early working with other drivers on our cars a full hour before we would be ready to go up into camp, pouring hot water in the radiators and turning over the frozen motors by crank. Their panting breaths congealed immediately and I reached for an extra sweater as I watched them heaving at our cars with little white plumes issuing from their mouths. Ignatz was still not wearing the wool-lined Army gloves I had scrounged for him; he considered them too elegant for work.

We drove up the long hill to the warehouse. Ignatz was quiet as usual. Except for a morning greeting, he seldom spoke unless spoken to and never a word about his personal life. Once when the other drivers had told me that he had a wife and two-year-old girl, he acted pained. He had accepted the clothes and sweets that I gave him with the slight blush of one who never believed that the world owed him anything.

"Shoes today, Ignatz," I said, thinking of the innumerable sacks of shoes we hoped to sort and size in a single day.

"Ja, ich weiss," said Ignatz, not taking his eyes from the road. He knew, as did the whole camp, that today we were starting on the precious shoeleather. Ordinarily, I reflected, he would have grinned slyly when reminding me that the camp always knew everything in advance of its happening. I looked at his sober profile, paler than usual.

We had unloaded the shoes in one of the stone stables that used to house a troop of Hitler's cavalry. On the wooden door was the sinister slant stencil of a shadow man with a brimmed hat pulled down over the ears, the Nazi's wordless warning on spies which decorated barn doors and house walls all over Germany. The warehouse crew waiting by the door must have been making jokes on the evil painted genie hovering over them. I saw Ignatz smile.

In the shoe shipment there were some two thousand pairs of old GI shoes. These tumbled from the sacks still bent to the shape of a foot that had walked from a Normandy beachhead into Germany. Many of the shoes were stiff with mud. We could knock this off by clapping together the stout soles. When the mud did not drop off easily, we knew that it had a tougher binder than water, that it was stuck to the shoes with a soldier's blood. Ignatz used a flat-bladed knife to scrape these clean of all but the stain.

Every time I walked down the rows where the GI shoes were being paired off in close formation along the cement floor, my throat constricted. When a pair had been set down pigeon-toed, I leaned over and straightened the stance to make it less eloquent of some tousle-headed kid fresh out of school and off to the wars.

Ignatz looked at the shoes with the eyes of an officer. He pointed to a pair with the patina of frequent shines still visible on the blunt boxed toes. "This one," he said, "good soldier" — as if, rising out of the empty shoetops, he clearly saw the unknown man who had tramped half across Europe and never neglected to shine his shoes each night in bivouac.

"Those men," I said sentimentally, "came to liberate you."

"*Warum?*" Ignatz's "why" was not impudent, it was a genuine question asked. His blue eyes flashed incredulity that anyone, a whole army of anyones, should have gone out of the way for the likes of him. How could one explain the nascent philosophy of international relief to one who had always stood on his own two feet and had never asked anything of the world except the right to live privately and in peace? In our peculiar pidgin I tried to tell Ignatz how we in America had felt when the Panzer divisions started rolling eastward, how we had looked at the newsreels of Hitler's blitz into Poland.

"*Kino.*" Ignatz shook his head. Never could cinema say how it really was. He slashed the tough stitching of a sack of size tens, up-ending it for the oncoming sorters. Then he put his index and middle fingers together like a pistol barrel and swung the hand in slow deliberation over all the bent forms in the warehouse, not missing one.

"Schiessen... schiessen... schiessen," he said sadly.

Shoot, shoot, shoot. The one word with its accompanying gesture was his total comment on the Germans. I could never trick him into saying more. Where he had been when the shooting was on, how he in the uniform of the flying corps had managed to escape extinction, I had not yet been able to learn. Six years of his talented young life lay folded away between the two bits of cardboard I had seen when he transferred the contents of his battered wallet to the new one I had bought for him from our mobile PX. The photograph of himself as a flying officer and his membership card in the organization of Former Prisoners of Concentration Camps had been exposed for a brief moment while he murmured *"Prima, prima"* for the new wallet.

We worked over the shoes until we were all shaking with fatigue. I tried to persuade Ignatz to go home with the other drivers at sundown but he shook his head and smiled gently. He would stay with Londa and me until we locked up. Maybe we would forget to lock up, as once we had done when we left a warehouse late at night.

When at last he was driving us down to our billets, Londa looked at the back of his shapely blond head and said:

"There's one lad who'll never owe a farthing to UNRRA for his maintenance meanwhile."

Ignatz jumped out of the car and held the door open for us, cap in hand like a driver serving royalty.

"For the sake of one like him," I said, "all the rest of this crazy work makes sense. You just need one like that and you can go on believing in the DP cause, no matter what the doctor says."

"I know what you mean," Londa said. "I've got one too. You'll meet him when he comes to my room for tea on Sunday. He's a shaven-headed ballet master. Once he danced with Pavlowa, he showed me his clippings. Of course, he's quite another dish than your Ignatz. I daresay there are quite a few who have kept their things intact, if only we could ever get around and really know our DP's."

"When we get snowed in."

"May God speed the day!" Londa went into the small room she occupied alone. I went on upstairs to the big front room I shared with the Belgian nurse. We called her Chouka, the Franco-Flemish diminutive that Marcel always used when calling his compatriot. The Venezuelan doctor was visiting with my roommate.

"Don't go, Pedro." I thrust his slight form back into the easy chair. "Let's have a drink before dinner."

We talked quietly in French, our common language. It was all shoptalk, a kind of unwinding that somehow seemed necessary before you could feel relaxed enough to approach food. Our big window framed the western sky already darkening to night except near the rim of the encircling hills where a silvery lightness lingered. Always at that hour when the first impersonal dark descended and a primeval silence settled over our remote corner of Bavaria, our talk about DP's sounded make-believe and unreal, as if we were just perversely imagining something that *could* happen to mankind if you didn't watch out... until a shot, a shout or a knock would bring the actuality into the room again. This time the tap on the door was made by fingers light and apologetic.

Ignatz stood in the opened door, at first unable to speak when he saw we had a guest in the room and thought he had interrupted a party. His agitated hands twisted his wool cap. The only color in his face was in the red rims of his eyes.

"Ignatz! *Was ist los?*"

He begged the car. He needed to go up to camp just for one small eye-blink of time. He would be right back. He must fetch a priest.

"Priest? What for?"

"Neues Kind tot." Two tears rolled down his face. His new baby was dead. We had not even known that he had a new baby or that the baby was ill.

Chouka and the doctor rose quickly from their chairs and followed me out the door with Ignatz. We stumbled over the dark back pathway, four houses up where our drivers lived. We climbed the bare stairs to the second-floor corner room that I had assigned to Ignatz from a blueprint but never visited, because he was so shy, so very private about his private life.

Ignatz held open the door of his room, gesturing us to precede him into the steamy sanctum that contained all he cherished on earth. In one startled glance I saw for the first time his young child-faced wife, the small daughter clinging in fright to her skirts, and the handmade crib in a corner of the room holding a high-puffed lace pillow with a tiny shape upon it so infinitesimally small that it made no indentation. The dead infant was already dressed for burial in a long white gown with blue ribbons run through the embroidered yoke. An immense organdy bonnet was pleated around an aged violet face no bigger than half my palm.

The Venezuelan doctor leaned over the crib and murmured in his own tongue, *"Prématura."* He touched the minute blue fingers through which a cotton lily had been drawn. Possibly a seven-month baby, he said, which should never have been taken from hospital inside of two or three months. He questioned Ignatz in a gentle professional way as his hands explored the birdlike anatomy. The infant had perished of malnutrition in its fifth week.

I thought of Ignatz during the past five weeks, day by day watching his son grow smaller if possible and never saying a word to any of us, his friends and neighbors. I thought of him as he had worked side by side with me tallying mountains of powdered milk and the heavier condensed cream that came in some of the Red Cross parcels, and never hinting that his wife could have used some of those tins. In fact, very often refusing at the end of those days the piece of vitaminized chocolate that I handed out to all the workers. You could only suppose that after the life he had led, he was so unused to asking for anything, even help, that the thought of asking never occurred to him.

Chouka was saying in a low shocked voice, "Ignatz, why didn't you come to us?" but it was only a rhetorical question. She knew that he could not have borne to have his wife and baby moved back to the hospital as she would promptly have ordered. Even as she asked the question, the little wife moved closer to her man in fright. Another dangerous separation threatened. Ignatz stood with his hands clasped in front of him like a culprit awaiting sentence.

Then he said, "Tonight, *Schwester,* can we keep him with us?" In his eyes was the knowledge of the dreary basement under Chouka's TB hospital that we used for the camp morgue. He had helped her hospital manager to pour cement and make a mortuary table so bodies would no longer have to lie upon the floor. He also knew the camp rules — prompt removal to the mortuary after death.

The doctor nodded permission and said to us in French, "After all, starvation is not contagious."

Chouka went over to the crib and lit the one white candle standing at its head on the window sill. The candle holder was a jam tin that Ignatz had cut and curled into a shiny decorative tray. Beside it stood the parts of a salvaged carburetor he was rebuilding for my car. He knew how to do absolutely everything — except ask for help.

Winter began that night as I tossed and turned on the wide bed built for a German officer, spread-eagling and retracting on its hard three-sectioned mattress, trying never to think of Ignatz keeping vigil over that crib and thinking of him continuously while trying to count GI shoes instead of sheep, counting them carefully pair by pair and cornering the stoutest-soled for the woodcutters, next stoutest for the truck drivers and warehousemen and so on down the long rows to the civilian shoes that American housewives had gathered up in response to radio appeals for clothing for those poor refugees overseas, noting as I counted the excellent pair of Spalding golf oxfords that one emotional housewife had probably taken from her husband's closet while he was at work (and caught hell for afterwards) and hearing Ignatz remark with delicate irony that those *prima* shoes would doubtless be seen on the feet of a committee big fish long before our strictly nonpreference distribution began... Your DP's are at it again, said the captain's voice over the phone from Military Government, they've raided another German farm. *My* DP's, why do you always say my DP's as if I had given birth to the whole Godforsaken pack of them? And why do you think it is always our Poles who raid those German farms? Didn't it ever occur to you that the German farmers often slaughter their cattle and sell the beef to their own people rather than sit around waiting for you to requisition it at one tenth the black market rate? (Ignatz goes goose-hunting with the car bumper, running right at the insolent hissing pack with me egging him on, but that's another question.) There was a nun walking in camp today leading a goat by a string but you wouldn't wonder for a moment about the goat, only about her pleated headpiece snowy white and starched in the middle of a soapless and starchless Germany... And while you're on the line, Captain, I'd like to ask why Army stupidly insists on dyeing those captured Wehrmacht ski pants from horizon blue to navy — a thousand pairs that would have been *prima* for our woodcutters, only they came back from your dye works shrunk to the size for a ten-year-old boy. I stole a pair for Ignatz anyhow, out of the undyed lot bundled for Army pick-up. He promised he would never wear them outside camp where your prowling patrols circulate. I don't know why we dare not offend German eyes with the sight of their captured army ski pants on their former slaves, do you?

"Why don't you sleep?" Chouka said from her mammoth bed in the opposite corner. "The baby would have died anyhow even if we'd have kept it in the hospital for glucose feeding."

"He so deserved a son."

"God disposes. Go to sleep."

Why then, I asked myself, had He not disposed of one of those illegitimate babies, unwanted and flourishing in ever-mounting statistics in our camp? Even being sold to the Germans if you could believe the gossip grapevine. Or throttled at birth. I thought of the baby that had been spilled out of an ashcan just the week before, a perfectly formed full-term male child with a faint lavender thumbprint on the front of its neck.

Sleep would not come. I reviewed the hunt for the guilty mother. Our nurses made house visits to every woman who had passed through the prenatal clinic or maternity hospital in that month, but a baby was found by the side of each. Then the Canadian said, But of course we're on the wrong track, the woman we want would never have asked us for help, would never have got her name on our books since she planned to destroy her child. She'd have delivered herself all alone, probably off in the woods somewhere. The uterus, said Chouka, will not be descended yet, we can find her by palpation. In any one of those twenty-eight hundred rooms? You're mad, I said, you'd be looking for a needle in a haystack. We'll find her if our feet hold out. *Cherchez la femme.* On the third day they brought the culprit to Pierre. She was the frightened young girl who had come to me on my first day of duty in the camp, bearing a note about Joe, her "fiancé" who had sowed his seed and gone Stateside and forgotten her completely except, no doubt, in his bragging. *Boy, once I had me a Polack babe...* Captain, we found her, the case of the ash barrel baby, you remember? She's not the monster we thought, just a frightened young girl, extenuating circumstances. We've got to turn her over to Mil Gov as an object lesson because we made such a stink with the Polish committee about camp morals, but tell me how I can write it up so she won't get sent to Intermediary Court in Schweinfurt. Ah, so that's the phrase. Temporarily deranged by the pain and agony of unassisted birth. Thank you, thank you, I'll do as much for you someday...

The first snow fell on Wildflecken that night. It dropped straight from a windless sky in fine flakes that built white pads on the pines and drifted softly over all the rough spots in the encircling hills. In the morning we looked out upon a skier's paradise of maddening beauty which made us forget momentarily our daily bread of grief and woe, as if this handsome act of Nature had transformed us into winter sports enthusiasts with not a care in the world but that the snow stay dry and powdery.

For once around the breakfast table, the DP's were as remote from the conversation as they would have been in a St. Moritz resort. We talked as if we had nothing to do except ski all winter or learn to ski.

"Baedeker calls these Rhön Mountains the poor man's Alps." Knut, our Norwegian supply man, generally the quiet one at the table, told about slalom races in Oslo and how he had spotted a slope behind the bakery which would be perfect for a starter. "I'll teach the beginners," he promised.

"Me, no," said Pedro. "I stay whole so I can set your broken bones." He said "brawken bawns" and we laughed with affection for his Spanish accent while feeling secure that he was one of our international family, an ace surgeon whose scarless stitching was performed with a delicate curved gold needle he had brought with him from Caracas.

Laughter and ski talk lit up the faces for play and you had to look twice to recognize your old teammates. Maybe all over Germany it was like that, I thought, with the first snows since war's end blanketing the rubble piles and giving briefly the illusion that they were not there at all, that the war had been only a nightmare from a troubled conscience. The mood was wonderful while it lasted. It lasted until someone happened to glance automatically out the window toward the railroad tracks.

The cattle cars shunting slowly into the station were the same as all the hundreds of others that had linked our days into weeks and weeks into months, in dismal repetitive continuity, except now the cars were thatched with glistening snow and icicles instead of homemade flags hung from the car corners.

"Maybe," said Knut wistfully, "it's only our coal shipment. We've got one due."

"Look again, slalom champ," said the Canadian nurse. "Since when do they install wood stoves in coal cars?"

Smoke from the stovepipes elbowing out from each car wrote the familiar hieroglyphics in the icy air. We read them and went into our act. Call the trucks. Alert Billeting. Stand by with hot soup for all and milk for pregnant and lactating mothers.

It was the same old team that hurried out the mess hall door. The row of butter knives at Knut's place, laid out in patterns for a stem Christy, a downhill run, an uphill climb, were all that remained of our St. Moritz mood.

~ 7 ~

You have to look through a block of ice to get the proper perspective on that first winter in Wildflecken. It has to be a clear block that does not distort the outlines of the twelve thousand Poles frozen in with the eighteen UNRRA men and women assigned to care for them. Surround that city-sized ice block with dense evergreen forests coated with frozen fog spun out glistening as far as eye can see and you have the fairy-tale world of Karl Grimm where we lived and labored for four snowbound months, minus of course the help of the fairies, whom History had displaced.

All life reduced to the stark simplicity of the supply line. Weekly boxcars of food and coal from Army depots in Würzburg appeared automatically in our railroad station, but the task of trucking the stuff one mile up our icebound hill to the warehouses haunted us before, during and after each operation. Often a thin glassy film of frozen fog lay over the cobbles, and until the pale sun came forth, not a thing could move on the deathtrap surface except the bedstead sleds our Poles had invented by sawing off the rounded tops of their iron beds and using these curved pieces as runners on their homemade inflexible flyers.

Food and fuels were the essentials of our supply anxieties but to round out our job a thousand other things were needed, and these we had to hunt for ourselves and take, when we found them, by any means including outright seizure, when barter with cigarettes and chocolate failed.

There was not, for example, a sewing machine needle in the whole of Germany — at least, not visible on any counter. Our Welfare had twelve sewing machines, the cornerstone for a sewing shop that would take our single women off the streets and give them useful employment if we could find needles for the machines. Londa and her French welfare girls went forth daily to scour cowtowns and villages within a radius of fifty miles.

Pedro was like a traveling salesman forever on the frozen road in quest of medicines and hospital equipment, following hints and rumors of some new dump of captured German medical supplies suddenly thrown open by Army to first-comers. When he returned to camp with such needed items as breast pumps, TB sputum cups and hypo needles, we feted him as for a birthday, after thawing him out.

Welding rod was another urgently needed item. Our Belgian engineer Jan discovered a broken snowplow and a welding machine side by side in an abandoned shed, but no welding rod. He became obsessed with the idea that the rod had to be somewhere in the camp. His calm Flemish nature altered in the weeks he hunted for it. He groped through unexplored warehouses until he was bleached like a snow man and racked with frustration, and all the other objects he unearthed by the way — unexpected treasures such as diesel engines packed in grease, man-high drums of copper wire worth its weight in gold, hundreds of pairs of canvas snowshoes with flexible wood soles — brought no light of joy to his maniacal eyes.

Everyone developed the balmy faraway look of the old prospector. The multiple sweaters, socks and wool pants we wore to combat the zero days carried out the derelict impression. Then a nurse, prospecting for baby scales, discovered a cache of tanned sheepskins in a closed furrier shop in a distant town, which she thought could be had in exchange for lard. When Jan located his welding rod and got the snowplow mended, he returned to normal and went forth to barter for the nurse's find. And presently we were all walking around in great sheepskin jackets with pointed hoods, with the leather on the outside dyed brown (to differentiate us from the DP's in their white shepherd coats) and the fleece on the inside curling out from under the hoods like the white hair of the aged.

Each month another ten-thousand-box edition of Red Cross food parcels was laid down in our railroad station, and now we had another group than the tender little scouts to open these in the arctic wastes of the warehouse, where every tin that was touched stuck to the fingers in the searing cold. Tak Tak Schön had told us about the *Société de Culture Physique,* a group of some forty prisoner-of-war women who had come to Wildflecken directly from Dachau, Buchenwald and Ravensburg and had been the camp's public women until a gifted Polish aristocrat had gathered them together in fierce possessive pride and created work for them to do to bring them back into society slowly and surely from lives that only she could understand, since she had been one with them in the concentration camp of Ravensburg. Before Ravensburg, the Countess told me, Madame Stanislawa had been a diplomaed engineer in Warsaw, a mathematician of repute and a belle of the old prewar society.

Madame Stanislawa marched her forty PW women to the food warehouse on a bitter December day when fine snow lay like sugar on the ground, every grain separate and dry. The women's tramping feet scuffed clouds behind their heels and the supply area looked like a smoking white battleground with those warrior women surging across it singing their brigade songs in voices from which all woman sounds had long since been tortured, raped and wept out. These were the women who had fought side by side with their men behind the Polish barricades, who had been captured by the Nazis, by the Russians and by Nazis again, as battle lines advanced and fell back, and who had been used by each conqueror as they passed from hand to hand. Their battered faces were charged with spirit as if release from their prisons had happened only yesterday.

Beside the boisterous column like a stern and watchful top sergeant walked the woman who had regenerated the group. Madame Stanislawa, Diplomaed Engineer, wore ski pants and a wool peasant blouse belted about a narrow waist. Her short cropped hair clung closely to a sculptured skull. Harsh lines of pain gave her face a forbidding look, until she spoke, and then her deep voice seemed to draw you behind the scenes, as it were, behind the pale unsmiling face and tragic eyes to the place where her single remaining emotion lived — her love for the tough unbeaten women whom she ruled with a hand of iron. They obeyed her like schoolgirls in love with their teacher.

The great warehouse drew audiences like a theater during the months the PW women worked there. Though the supply area was off limits to all except authorized employees, there was always a crowd of delighted Poles peering through the barred windows, and every truck that backed inside the warehouse to load up with the supplemental ration for that day had a dozen volunteer helpers aboard. The men who had come to look at their old flames at work were greeted with raucous shouts from the women and often a pointed remark that would send some hulking peasant hurrying out the door with red ears. There was continuous laughter and hoarse singing and a volume of production we had never seen before.

We gave the women broken packages of cigarettes to smoke and kept gallons of hot soup for them on the two iron stoves we had had installed. Londa brought from her clothing warehouse some dyed Wehrmacht ski jackets, originally destined for men workers but shrunk to woman size in the dyeing. Each time we thought of something else to do for her magnificent Magdalenes, Stanislawa walked away behind the stacked boxes so they would not see her face of joy.

Every day around four, as darkness was falling, Stanislawa gave the order to start burning the emptied Red Cross boxes. This was the wild finale for which all the men workers in the supply area waited. More than a thousand boxes were flung to the flames that leaped fifty feet high in the freezing dusk, a beacon that told the camp that another big *pakiety* day had ended. Snow fell through the roaring radiance and the women with their swollen red hands and shining faces pranced around their gigantic bonfire in rowdy release from their exacting toil. Then the first snowball would be thrown, spinning into the firelight from the outer circle where Polish guards and truck drivers clustered. The fight was on, tough man-girl roughhouse with bodies pinned down in snow and the air thick with shouts and cries and glistening missiles that exploded in white showers against shawled heads silhouetted by the blaze.

When Marcel came up with the taxi trucks, our wrestling warrior women climbed aboard and shook out their shawls demurely. Stanislawa made sure that all forty were safe in the two trucks before she climbed up with Marcel to lead her robust flock homeward to the rooms she shared watchfully with them.

As snow and ice sealed us off from the outside world, we penetrated deeper into the camp and the lives of our people. Every hour not given to crisis or sudden arrival was occupied with block-visiting. We had some twenty-eight hundred rooms in the camp in which the Poles were settling in for their winter in Slavic style. They nailed windows to stay shut until spring, bound babies like papooses in endless unhealthy yards of woolen swaddling clothes, and swung ever-burdened clotheslines in the crowded interiors to produce, as our medical people said sadly, the proper incubating steam for swift transmission of respiratory diseases.

Block-visiting was a queer haunting business. You never knew, when you stood in the dim central hallways running the length of a blockhouse, with your hand on a grimy doorknob, what the opening of that door was going to reveal. A card on the door gave the number of square feet and the names of the individual souls the room contained, but that was no preparation. The entire scale of the human condition could be in any single room, or just one happy or forlorn note of it. It might be a bachelors' room bleak and bare with forty iron beds spaced at intervals along the walls and an ugly German army wardrobe standing narrow and tall beside each bed. Or, it might be a room where two or three families from the same village in Poland had managed to get together to create with ikons, oleographs and lace bedspreads a semblance of the homes they had left behind.

Most generally it would be a room into which the billeting committee had thrust heterogeneous families according to their size, with the old-timers secure by the windows and the newcomers in the dim spaces along the windowless walls. These were the rooms that always caught at one's heart, for they were partitioned off into family cubicles with the narrow wardrobes and stacked luggage built together to make one dividing wall, and Army blankets hung from ropes to close in the remaining footage authorized to each.

You stared at these khaki labyrinths, the last ramparts of privacy to which the DP's clung, preferring to shiver with one less blanket on their straw-filled sacks rather than to dress, comb their hair, feed the baby or make a new one with ten to twenty pairs of stranger eyes watching every move. You knew then that no matter what had happened to these people in the merciless herdings of them from homeland to enemy land, there was this one thing that could never be taken from them — the sense of privacy, the essence of human dignity.

Rising from the blanket-hung cubicles was a fixed medley of sounds descriptive of the private life each contained — a moan of concertina, the tap-tap of a jeweler's hammer, the wail of a baby, the whirr of a sewing machine. Over all hung a redolent cloud of atmosphere composed of differing elements in the different communal rooms, but always smelling the same, a synthesis of drying diapers, smoked fish, cabbage brews and wood smoke from wet pine. It was not an unpleasant smell once you got used to it. For us it became the identifying odor of homeless humanity.

Always when you were looking for some specific person in these labyrinthine rooms, you visited first in the open space around the community stove that burned night and day and at all hours was covered with the pots of each family's food, which was brought in pails from the central kitchens and improved indoors with bits of meat or vegetables procured in that day's bartering. This open space in the partitioned rooms gave the peculiar impression of an inside public square to which drifted the inmates of the surrounding blanket-town when they got lonely, cold or hungry. Here was gossip, cooking, boot- and diaper-drying and all the other business that man has ever performed before a fire. Here also could always be found someone with the soul of a concierge who could lead you through the maze of woolen-walled corridors to the room within a room that you were seeking, telling you meanwhile every detail of what went on behind that particular khaki curtain.

As winter progressed, we became interested mainly in seeing what was cooking on the communal stoves. We were spot-checking for steaks.

Increasingly we had been receiving from an irate Military Government reports of livestock missing from German farms. Army threatened us with a raid if we did not locate and suppress the meat black market which they said was flourishing in our camp. At first we indignantly denied this possibility. Why, we asked our accusers, should our Poles risk raiding German farms when Red Cross parcels were coming into camp every month to add almost daily to the regular ration some such blood-warming extra as a tin of salmon per person? Nobody was acutely hungry any more, we said.

But what we did not know, what was virtually impossible for us to realize, with the food parcel strike still bright in the memory, was that our Poles were not used to the highly concentrated Red Cross foods and were hungering for something they could really get their teeth into. Like fresh beef.

Skeptically we added steaks to the long list of reasons for inspecting our DP living quarters and we spent freezing hours in blockhouse basements where every other animal sound except the mooing of a cow could be heard. Ducks, chickens, rabbits and guinea pigs had been brought indoors to winter in these subterranean barnyards. Sometimes our flashlights would ring a fur-capped farmer just squatting there in the gloom staring at a pair of spectral geese and ruminating, no doubt, on some plot of land beyond the River Bug to which he could never return.

It all looked innocent, bucolic and slightly sad until one day Londa's exploring flashlight fell full on the horns and hoofs of what had been a cow. The swift butchering had just been accomplished. The stone floor was still wet from a recent scrubbing, but beyond the dim corner stall there was not a trace in any direction to show where the meat had gone. There was not a drop of blood, a tuft of hide or a sliver of bone anywhere on stairs or corridors of the vast blockhouse. Most puzzling of all, there was not a hoofprint in the snow outside, although the week's story of the in-and-out traffic of humans, dogs, skiers and sledders was clearly stamped there in the deep hard crust.

We might have seen the far-reaching effects of the first official carcass hunts in our camp if there had not been something slightly comical about them. We might have realized that here was the beginning of a legend that would cling to the DP's for the rest of their days, that they were nothing more than a looting horde sitting pretty under the protection of UNRRA and free to make sorties on the poor frightened Germans any time that life in the camp became too dull.

The first seizure by Army was made right at our own main gate out of a truck with the UNRRA symbol on its hood. It was a taxi truck which ran several times daily from camp to railroad station, so familiar to the GI gate guard that he generally waved it through without inspection. But one evening it halted at the barrier with something hanging out the back of it, something that looked like a piece of rope well raveled at the tip, until it lifted, curled and fell back. The guard peered into the covered truck at the prone body of a live cow which the Polish driver and his assistant had somehow managed to hoist aboard, truss down and cover neatly with blankets and sacks. All they forgot to do was tuck in the tail.

The next time, Army came in hot pursuit directly into camp to the door of a specific blockhouse where two pigs, shot the night before on a German farm, were reported hidden by the marauders. The DP informer (who probably had not been promised his cut of pork) accompanied the search party. Our captain from Military Government went from attic to basement of the blockhouse poking into every room, every wardrobe, every crate and sack, with Pierre and me trotting at his heels like anxious parents. The captain even inspected the men's and women's toilets at each end of the long hallways. I did not learn until long afterwards that the two old ladies we had intruded upon in the women's toilets, crouched over the seats with shawled heads bent low and elbows on their knees, were the two pig carcasses we sought, dressed and posed with such imaginative realism that even our captain had leaped back in embarrassment when I had pulled open the latrine doors.

The third search involved the newly revived German police, stiff and formal in their field-green uniforms and full of certainty that this time they would find their cow and prove to us meddling foreigners that all we were harboring was a crowd of cattle thieves.

Ignatz drove me, with Kowalski, our new chief of DP police, to a nearby village where the cow tracks started, leading off from a sod-roofed barn across snow meadows to the outer fringe of woods surrounding our camp. It seemed to me that with the honor of the Poles at stake, Ignatz and Kowalski were singularly lighthearted as we plodded through the woods with the German police. The big bifurcated hoof-prints of the stolen cow made a clear and incriminating trail that was going to enter the camp, I observed nervously, in the region of the blockhouse where Londa had once stumbled over the horny remnants of the mystery cow that had apparently flown into camp on wings.

Ignatz and Kowalski talked sociably together in Polish like two sportsmen out for a stroll, pausing now and again to examine rabbit tracks criss-crossing the posthole prints in the icy crust which marched like doom toward the camp. Kowalski's unconcern puzzled me. His cherished job as police chief would end the moment those cow tracks crossed the Wildflecken boundary. I thought of all the other times when, in the absence of Pierre, I had accompanied Kowalski on a mission of law and order. I had seen him shooting up schnapps stills, tracking down petty thieves, weeding out political agitators — all with the gusto of a character out of a Wild West story, which indeed he seemed to be, the lone pistol-packing Pole (by special permission of Division H.Q.) who always got his man.

This time, Kowalski was the one who would be had. I knew how those two angry Germans plodding beside me through the snow would make him pay. Every German policeman in that corner of Bavaria was out to get this exuberant Pole in retaliation for the side show he had recently staged with two German women whom he had caught trafficking in cigarettes in the camp. Before turning the arrested women over to the proper outside authorities, Kowalski had set them to scrubbing the floors of his police headquarters, meanwhile inviting in the camp inhabitants to have a good long look at their former conquerors down on their knees beside a scrub bucket.

"Bitte schön, Frau Direktor, sehen Sie hier." One of the German police stopped to point to a brown spot of cow dung recently dropped across the trail. I nodded and tried to look ashamed for my Poles. Ahead, I could see the sagging single wire which marked the perimeter of Wildflecken.

At a precise spot just a few dozen yards our side of the wire, the cow tracks vanished utterly. There were the four deep prints where the cow had last stood and then, ahead of these, nothing but smooth snow with its solid ice crust stretching down an aisle of pines into the camp.

I stared, as astonished as the Germans. It was as if right there some supernatural force had yanked the cow straight into the air. Involuntarily the Germans glanced up at the evergreen boughs overhead. They held a conference, muttering rapidly together with exclamations like *"Verdammt!"* and *"Sonderbar!"* escaping clear from their consternation.

Ignatz and Kowalski stood aside respectfully, watching them examine the snow under all the bushes around as if maybe right there the cow had shrunk to something of rabbit size. I looked under a few bushes myself just to appear co-operative. Then, for my own bedeviled curiosity, I examined the hard-packed snow beyond the last four foot-holes. But there was no evidence of spadework smoothing.

We walked in silence back to our cars. I gave a sympathetic *Auf Wiedersehen* to the Germans and waited until they had jeeped out of sight. Then I looked Kowalski straight in the eye and said, "Now you tell me."

"But what, Frau Direktor? You were there. You saw."

Kowalski's blue eyes brimmed with laughter while he tried to make his big pink face look perplexed. Ignatz kept his eyes to the road, driving with a concentration that the straightaway hardly required. I saw that I would get nothing from either of them and would have to live with the mystery of the vanishing cow until the explanation filtered through from some other source.

Eventually one of our bachelor teammates picked up the story that was too good to be kept. His source was much closer to the heart of the Poles than any contacts I enjoyed. It was his willowy blond Polish mistress who explained to him how the DP's had made from sacks immense padded carpet slippers which they had put on the cow's four feet at the point of the disappearing footprints, and thus had led the beast without trace into the camp.

~ 8 ~

If the Poles had not begun chopping down the evergreens around their blockhouses, we probably never would have realized that Christmas was so near. We saw them trudging through snowy camp streets with small spruces under their arms, with bigger ones being dragged on the bedstead sleds, and sometimes with a tree so tall it took two men to haul it along. We could not imagine where in the crowded blockhouses space would be found for those Christmas trees, but it was evident that every family intended to condense into that first Christmas after liberation all the missed celebrations of the preceding six years of slavery.

Schnapps stills sprouted up faster than Kowalski could shoot them down and confiscate their copper coils, and any small segment of coil left undiscovered seemed to have earthworm ability to reproduce itself endlessly. The stills diminished from corporation size to little family affairs that could be operated in the privacy of the rooms like coffee percolators. Our doctors set aside a special ward in one of the hospitals to accommodate the cases of facial burns on Poles whose last memory, before the explosion, was of peering into their homemade stills to see how things were bubbling along.

The Christmas spirit was like a living presence pervading everything in the camp except us. We were moving too fast to keep up with it to be caught by it, but it touched us everywhere in passing — in the look of blockhouse doorways transfigured by chromos of the Christ child framed in evergreen, in the practice sounds from Slavic choral groups which surged in splendor from clubroom windows, in the queer new smell in some of the DP rooms which aesthetic inmates were whitewashing with powdered milk to make them beautiful for the holidays, until we stopped that practice by ordering them to drink their milk and threatening to have it mixed in the central kitchens if they persisted in their interior decorating.

Ten days before Christmas, we were sure that the momentum of holiday events had reached its peak. Two men on the team turned bright yellow with the jaundice of fatigue and had to be hospitalized. We had three boxcars of coal and five boxcars of food sitting on our railroad siding and barely enough gasoline to haul this bonanza up to what was no longer the safety of the warehouses. From the small stone cigarette warehouse where a GI guard (loaned to us from a neighboring tank battalion) slept each night, we discovered one thousand packages of cigarettes missing, and from another warehouse a load of soap had vanished including the truck it had arrived in, which we had not had time to tally in and had left standing loaded inside the barred and padlocked door.

We solved the cigarette loss easily because it was another story too good to be kept. Through a hole in the base of the warehouse door, our Poles had thrust a bottle of their Christmas schnapps and had serenaded the imbibing GI with concertina music and sweet voices of women on the outside urging him to push out the key. Not being a man of iron, he had pushed out the key.

The soap theft was insoluble. The soap truck reappeared in the ranks of our motor pool, scrupulously washed and polished as if its phantom driver had desired to show gratitude to UNRRA for the loan of transport. All that was certain was that our DP police had had to be in connivance. So we went through the anxious business of selecting (for the third time since we had taken over the camp) a brand-new security guard and we changed the police overnight in a surprise move, retaining only Kowalski the chief, who had established his alibi with tears of rage for the defection of his men.

"Now," said Pierre, "nothing more can happen. With new police, I can be tranquil during my Christmas vacation in Paris."

"They'll be good boys until spring," I said, counting on my fingers. They would begin with virtuous zeal as had their predecessors. They would allow only a few chosen friends to fish at night with long hooked wires lowered through the high broken windows of the clothing warehouse and only a few overcoats would be missing at first. For a time they would be savagely strict about the portage of cigarettes from the Red Cross warehouse to the stone stable vaults (where a new American soldier on loan had not yet heard the song of the Slavic sirens), and first discrepancies between tally out and tally in would be slight. Then the disappearances would mount. You could almost plot it on a chart. It seemed to take about three months for a new outfit to get into its full stride when losses could be computed by the sackful and crateload. Meanwhile, it gave one a comfortable feeling to be starting the Christmas season with a fresh group of guards who would not risk loss of the military greatcoats that went with their jobs until they had exploited to the last brass button the courting advantages their uniforms gave them over all other cavaliers in the camp.

On Friday the twenty-first of December I waved good-by to Pierre and five other Continentals who were taking Christmas leaves at home in France, Holland and Belgium. They had all hoarded their PX chocolate, cigarettes and American store clothing to take to their famished families and their truck was loaded to its canvas top with bundles of the only civilian Christmas cheer that moved on the continent of Europe that year, like rich blood out from its renewed heartland — the Santa Claus world of the U.S. Zone of Occupation.

"Au revoir, Madame la Directrice!" Pierre wiped his eyes and pulled over his bald head the sheepskin hood that was going to set a new style on the Champs-Elysées.

"Joyeux Noël!"

I watched the truck skid crabwise down the glazed hill until it disappeared over the edge of our frozen planet, feeling not at all like a director in charge of operations, but more like the Old

Woman Who Lived in a Shoe. Then I hurried back to camp to see what our twelve thousand children were up to now.

Few of us went to bed at all during the forty-eight hours of that week end preceding the Tuesday Christmas of 1945. Over the Saturday and Sunday we had to issue to our Poles the food and fuel to keep them alive until the twenty-seventh, because their sacred trio of holidays began on the twenty-fourth and went through the twenty-sixth, which was the Feast of St. Stephen, the first Christian martyr, who was stoned to death. Not a Pole would work on any of those holy days. The furious scene of preparation for them, the Central Supply Area, was now an acre of solid ice surrounded by snow-capped warehouses and backdropped on all sides by tall pines that our last storm had transformed into trees of glass.

Many times before, I thought I had seen the supply area at its apogee — when tons of clothing had been dumped into it on rainswept November nights, when the scouts took possession of it with song, when Stanislawa's PW women marched across it as to war. But that Christmas week end I saw it lifted so high out of the humdrum and whirling with such activity that it seemed to exist apart like a dangerously spinning satellite wrenched free of the camp it served as central feeding organ, feeding it now through lines of such infinite attenuation that it was almost as if the food were being sprayed through space downward to where the people waited.

Stanislawa commanded the Red Cross warehouse, where a hundred scouts and her PW women were tearing open twelve thousand food parcels, storing the fish, fat and meat contents and leaving nine items in each *pakiety,* fancy foods like raisins, biscuits, tea, coffee and liver paste — the individual Christmas present for each camp inhabitant which in a moment of godmotherly aberration I had received permission to give to our DP's. These partially emptied boxes were even separated by gender — chocolate left in the boxes for females, cigarettes left in the boxes for males, and from every box that we would deliver into DP hands the Red Cross symbol had to be ripped, clawed or scraped off because we had no black ink for fast effacement of it.

Every bedstead sled in camp had been borrowed from the children to transport the Christmas boxes since we were too short of gasoline to use the trucks. Leaders from the sixty blockhouses, each with five helpers, came to the supply area early Saturday dragging strings of sleds, pushing baby buggies and kiddy-carts, and where a blockhouse lacked such mobile equipment, its messengers marched in with sacks, blankets and even lace bedspreads to be filled. These three hundred human carriers were admitted to the warehouse at first by individual house group, after Tak Tak Schön had identified their leader as the lawful man to collect three or four hundred boxes. Stanislawa, on the inside, snatched the official paper showing how many males, how many females in each house, called to the scouts to start loading, and, since no group could carry away its authorized total on one trip but had to return again and again, she set up a kind of mystic bookkeeping, half in her head, half on bits of paper, so that she knew the number of boxes due each returning group just by looking at the face of its leader, and presently she was loading two or three groups at a time so as not to keep the others immobile too long in the freezing cold outside. Then the only words she spoke were numbers.

Doubling, trebling, quadrupling her simultaneous servings, she stood like stone driving the streams back outward faster and faster with their loads until the motion engendered in her forceful fixity flowed out over the whole supply area and turned it into a tossing sea of boxes piled so high on sleds, buggies, and in packs on human backs that you could no longer see the vehicles bearing the teetering loads, but only the direction of their flow over the ice downhill toward camp.

This went on for two days and far into the nights and was only one current of the supply area activity. From the main food warehouse truckloads of lard, flour and meat groaned downward in low gear toward the twelve camp kitchens, and from the huge stockpile of cut logs by the sawmill the firewood trucks backed off with perilous loads. Every time these food and fuel trucks started skidding toward my ant-lines of bedstead sleds and baby buggies, the Poles laughed and shouted because everything was gorgeous and dangerous and some of the waiting groups even kept warm by sledding in front of the trucks like dolphin sporting before ships' bows.

When dark descended at four each afternoon, scores of bonfires burgeoned over the ice and were fed higher and higher with the spilled logs from firewood trucks until the cherry glow spread to the farthest fences and multiplied by its shadow every bundled shape in the area so that it seemed as if the whole camp had moved up to that frozen acre of chaos in chiaroscuro. Sometimes I detected a team member hurrying between fires and called for news in other departments. UNRRA people could be distinguished in the milling horde since Marcel had found *crampons* for each and had shod our rubber-soled Army shoes with these steel heel prongs that gave us a forward-tilting stride. The Canadian nurse paused to tell me she had admitted seven new pregnancies to her overcrowded Maternity and was frantically hunting spare sheets in the sewing shop. Chouka stumped through the scene seeking our Belgian engineer with an eleventh-hour request to have locks put on the windows of her TB hospital, from which her open cases were escaping down ropes of knotted sheets to rejoin their families in the blockhouses over the holidays and give them presents of Bacilli Koch.

Near midnight on Sunday the twenty-third, Stanislawa began counting out the Christmas boxes for the last of our blockhouses. She had sent the scouts home to bed and only her PW women remained in the cardboard shambles of the warehouse. I stood beside her mute with admiration while she watched the last block leader load his string of sleds. I wondered what she would do if I yielded to my impulse to put my arms around her thin shoulders and embrace her for the impossible job she had accomplished. But, like her PW women who gazed at her as into a mirror while they knotted head scarves wearily under blue chattering chins, I dared embrace her only with my eyes. As she rolled down her sleeve over the tattooed bone of her wrist, I glanced at her concentration-camp brand, the souvenir from what was probably the last pair of hands that had reached through her atmosphere of silence to touch her.

I walked with her at the side of her marching column across the deserted supply area to the gate, to make sure the DP guard would let her women pass through with the packages of cigarettes I had given to each. The area was a tide-land of moonlit ice strewn with the debris of flapping paper and broken crates, polka-dotted with black rings where bonfires had been. The wild waves of life that had surged over it had receded to the blockhouses below, whose windows showed through the pines, lit from attics to basements, vibrant with preparations that would continue until the last family cake was baked, the last family tree decorated.

Stanislawa stared ahead at the bright windows as at enemy territory, planning aloud her campaign against the loneliness her solitary women might feel if she did not keep them busy through what remained of the night.

"Now," she said sternly, "they will finish their rag dolls for the children in hospitals."

"Sto-lat... sto-lat..." An echo of the wonderful Polish drinking song floated up from one of the doorways where lusty males were sampling each other's home-brew.

"Rag dolls," replied Stanislawa to the bibulous woman-hunting echoes. "Nearly one hundred they have made already."

With no song left in them, her PW women tramped silently along hugging their cigarettes. Just once, at the gate, they came alive, when with husky cracks of laughter they shook their bundles of cigarettes under the nose of the envious guard and threatened him with their horny red hands.

I waited until they had trudged out of sight; then I got into my car and drove slowly down to the billets feeling as if I were coming home from all the wars. This time I had used up my second wind, which seemed to give some kind of instinctive assurance that nothing more could happen.

Chouka had propped up a Deutschepost telegram under the single small light left burning in the room. I had not expected Pierre to report with such touching promptness his safe arrival in

Paris. I slit the envelope and read the sender's address — UNRRA Regional Office, Bamberg. Then, unbelievingly, I read the peculiar typescript announcing our Christmas present from our organization:

> looo Pols beeing schipped 26th from Passau.
> Will trye advis exacte arrival.

The Signal Corps field phone seemed to have gone to bed with me. I battled it in my dreams as I was going to battle it most of the next day. Listen, listen, I've got to get through to Hickory, it's urgent. Hickory through Danube through Dagwood. Bamberg, Bamberg, can you hear me? You cannot, repeat not, send those Poles on the twenty-sixth. No, no, not Christmas hangover, it's a holy day, feast of St. Stephen, and if that's a Polish camp they're coming from, not a hand will be lifted there that day either so how could you load the transport? Load on the twenty-seventh and we'll receive the twenty-eighth. No, the twenty-seventh is a day like any other day. OK then, OK.

The Christmas parties... You must pick up that lovely device called a kaleidoscope, look down its cardboard barrel and turn it slowly against the light, watching the bits of brightness fall together and burst apart in wheeling sequences of stars and flowers, to see those Wildflecken celebrations as I did. The trembling shining fixity of each brief participation makes a chain of colored designs that spill through the memory to the tune of mazurkas and polkas and the faces of all the people I loved are in that twinkling moving field. I see Stanislawa's PW women exhausting their dance partners at the masked ball and eighty live dolls holding hands and playing ring-around-the-rosy in the kindergarten around a giant spruce gleaming with transformed tin-can ornaments... The barest twist and a blanket-walled cubicle falls together enclosing a village of grannies too old to dance but not to stare with child eyes at an immense Christmas cake iced in poison colors and topped by a candy house with cookies for paving stones over the sugar snow sprinkled before its chocolate-bar door...

There were too many parties. We were hardly enough to cover them all. *You take the warehouse and supply area wing-dings. You do the hospitals and the canteen celebrations. Can you cover the police, the truck drivers' and wood choppers' balls?* No party really came alive until the UNRRA officer appeared, no food was touched, no punch was poured. I tried to cover a bit of them all in my effort to replace the inexhaustible Pierre, who was missing the wildest show that our wild place had ever staged. I felt sorry for him with nothing more exciting to fill his Christmas holidays than the wooing of a bride, as he had whispered to me at parting. Poor Pierre, I thought, counting the thirty-fifth waltz whirl without a reverse that the Countess was making in the arms of Tak Tak Schön and neither of them falling flat on the floor when the music stopped. Poor Pierre... he'll miss the incoming transport from Passau, too. Coming in on a day like any other day... that is, I reflected, if our Poles can ever again settle down after this.

Just a day like any other day turned out to be the top-secret date of Third Army's first great search-and-seizure workout in the U.S. Zone, when, simultaneously, every DP camp was surrounded and house to house searches were made for the nameless treasures which the refugees were alleged to have amassed, like choosy connoisseurs, under our benevolent protection. The surprise raid was called "Tally-ho" and it began to move into Wildflecken at dawn on the twenty-seventh while we were still tossing in our dreams, exhausted by our ceaseless rounds of DP Christmas parties.

While we slept, GI's in fur-lined parkas began creeping through snow in pitch-black woods toward the fan-shaped boundary of the camp, sweeping every foot of ground with mine detectors that sought the caches of guns and ammunition presumed buried in the woods by plotting DP's. While these foot soldiers crept and swept inward from the hills, long lines of half-tracks, gun carriers, tanks equipped with walkie-talkies and trucks filled with helmeted infantrymen were grinding up our snow-muted hill from the main gate.

At six-thirty, just one half-hour before the raid would start, UNRRA was informed. I crawled cursing from my bed to answer the knock on my door.

"Who's there?" I quavered through the keyhole.

The familiar voice of the captain of our local tank battalion answered. I peered out at the splendor of his battle array — shellacked helmet, bulging pistol holsters and high-laced campaign boots — and thought, There is nothing more handsome than a tank battalion man dressed for business, as I led him into the disordered bedroom and lit the smallest light I could find.

"I'm sorry we couldn't tell you before." He looked away politely while I removed a hideous German hair net from my worn waves. "It was top secret. The camp is surrounded. It's Tally-ho."

"Tally-ho," I repeated to prove I was awake.

"Since three this morning the troops and tanks have been rolling into camp, main parts of two infantry divisions," he said quietly. "We'll arrest every DP without proper papers. We've set up two summary courts, one to try improper papers, one for illegal goods. The captain from Mil Gov will run the courts. He'll need you to identify pass violators."

He leaned forward as if to see what I was doing to my chin. I was holding it to the upper jaw so he would not hear my teeth chattering.

"Be prepared to have your camp paralyzed till sometime late this afternoon, everyone confined to his block until we clear his papers. Can you make out?"

I made out the shape of a bottle of gin. Maybe that would stop the rattling teeth.

"Like a drink?" I said. "Kind of a weird hour, but still..."

"You do good to have any Christmas ration left." He took a drink and poured one for me.

"Fifty-two truck drivers, a hundred and twelve bakers, a hundred and twenty policemen..." I counted the remainder of our thousand workers in my head and tried to imagine Wildflecken standing stock-still for eight or nine hours.

"Everyone," said the captain. "We've got to inspect papers of every single inhabitant."

"Do you expect trouble?" My fingers shook as I started to lace my field shoes.

"I don't know. What do you think?"

"I never think before sunrise."

"My boys have had a stiff briefing. If anyone gets trigger-happy..." He stood up and saluted. "Mil Gov has taken over the police block. Try to get up there as soon as you can. Get the team at their posts in hospitals, warehouses, workshops..."

Paul Revere never saw the sights that I saw as I rushed through the dark rapping on UNRRA doors. Because not until 1945 had there ever been a Christmas that was six Christmases rolled into one with twelve thousand Poles celebrating it and a scant dozen United Nations caretakers recovering from their supervision of it. The Norwegians had hangovers that only the descendants of Vikings could stand up with. A transport officer appeared at his door clad in long wool underwear and battle jacket and what I thought was a yellow lace hat on his head until I saw it was the hair of his taller mistress, who was hiding behind his back. Londa appeared in the black ballet tights in which she took dance instruction from Pavlowa's former partner and used as sleeping garment on zero nights. Our dyspeptic medical captain was a death's-head in the crack of his door after having been, to our astonishment, the *succès fou* of every polka-prancing party in the camp.

Ignatz peered out with the face of fright that the soldiers would see when they began knocking on blockhouse doors waking memories of Polish nights when the sound of knuckles had meant the NKVD or the Gestapo.

I did not know whether to laugh or cry as Ignatz sped me through ghostly camp streets from which the realistic Army maneuver had scared every DP including the dogs. Miles of motorized equipment lined the frozen roads. Light tanks with huge antennae waving aloft prowled about with their helmeted occupants talking tensely into field phones. There were enough

GI's in battle regalia to surround every blockhouse, with squads left over to man the machine guns set up on tripods before each decorated doorway. I looked at the gun barrels swiveling tentatively toward the only faces visible in the predawn dark, the chromos of the Christ child peering out from evergreen garlands.

I didn't see a DP until I entered the police block. Then I saw the camp's early risers — kitchen chefs, warehousemen, day-shift hospital workers — penned up en masse in the guardroom, before which stood an American sentry bursting with pride for the first fine catch of the day. His smooth young face was stern with certainty that every "character" held in detention by his broad back was an escaped Nazi storm trooper disguised as a DP.

"I suppose they all left their papers at home safely locked up in the little tin trunk," I said as calmly as I could. I looked over the sentry's shoulder at the scared faces of faithful workers who had been chased and cornered in the early dawn by jeeps and light tanks and who could think that nothing less than a third world war had started.

"That's what *they* say!"

His faint sneer sent me into the pass violators' court ready to take on singlehanded the two divisions of American Army that had frightened the daylights out of our DP's. The captain from Military Government was waiting for me, with his sergeant already at work booking prisoners queued up before the judgment desk.

"Don't gloat," I said to my captain friend. "I know every one of these people. I'll get them out as fast as your eager-beaver patrols bring them in."

"Take it easy. We've got a long long day ahead of us." His eyes glinted in anticipation.

"And a thundering herd of stolen cows you're hoping to find."

"From early indications, there ought to be plenty of stuff," he said with a grin. "I'll call you if we need to have goods identified." He stepped into the room next to mine, the happy hunting grounds of his black market court.

It was like sitting in tribunal and having members of a vast and never-ending family brought before you for judgment. Fear altered the known faces so you could not place them until they had mumbled some identifying frame-word like "kindergarten," "sawmill" or "warehouse." Until we had queried and freed the first groups of DP's and returned them to their surrounded blockhouses to fetch their identity cards and incidentally to spread the glad tidings that this was no war, only an *Ausweis-Kontrolle,* the air was tense with panic. At first the arrested ones spoke in such small choked voices, I had to thrust my face almost into their beards or shawls to catch their words. Then Ignatz brought the Countess to me, and when her strong familiar voice was heard by the prisoners, reciting back the old familiar litany of their mishaps with lost, stolen, burned or misplaced identity cards, the tension eased. After an hour or so even a little smothered laughter was heard, when patrols began bringing in the courting cavaliers found hiding in the wardrobes of blockhouses assigned to unmarried women.

The sergeant, who had never before worked with DP's, listened to my translations of their stories like a country boy agape before a sideshow barker. He freed every person whom I cleared, bringing his rubber stamp down with hypnotic obedience and occasionally muttering gratefully, "I'm sure glad someone can tell 'em apart, they all look alike to me."

Sounds of wailing and expostulation came from the captain's court but I could not go to see what he was doing until Londa came to relieve me at the pass desk.

"Watch out for Chouka's TB cases," I told her. "We've picked up three already and sent them back to hospital under guard. They'll try telling you they lost their cards but Chouka has them locked up. Here's the TB patient list for quick referral."

"I'm glad *something* good is coming out of this idiotic show," Londa said. "Really, you'd think the Battle of the Bulge was going on out there in the camp."

I looked quickly at the sergeant to remind her that Army was present and this was no time for us civilians to air our views on the military mentation.

A low chorus of lamentation came through the door giving into the black market court.

"What's *that* wailing wall?" Londa's angry eyes flashed toward the half-open door as I went through it.

I had moved with such precipitation into the captain's courtroom that I thought for an instant I had overshot my mark and landed up in the Red Cross warehouse. I stared in stupefaction at stacks of packaged foodstuffs covering all the tables of what was customarily the mess hall of the DP police, noting the neat segregation of products — a table for Jack Frost sugar, a table for Sun Maid raisins, a table for liver paste, a table for Nescafé — the unconsumed remainders of the Christmas present stuff that had gone out of the icy supply area three days before piled high on bedstead sleds, on human backs and in baby buggies. The backdrop of this supermarket display was a frieze of culprits around the walls on all three sides of the room which faced the judgment desk, flattened so tightly against the walls that they looked like bodies in bas relief frozen into hand-wringing postures of woe.

"My God, my God," was all I could say and I was not even sure that any sound came out of me because I felt something bursting in my head, like a vein or a clot or maybe the whole frontal lobe of the brain.

But the captain must have heard the single different note I had added to the one-keyed chorus of whimpers and moans that came from the fixed lips in the frieze around the walls and filled the room with a strange nonhuman intonation as if marble mourned.

He swung around quickly on his judgment seat and showed me the face of Julius Caesar home from campaigns in all three parts of Gaul with enough loot to keep a Roman populace quiet until the new moon. His smile had the pure lofty look of justice. Only a sardonic twist at the corners of his handsome mouth reminded me of all our wars of words over the telephone every time some snuffling German had stood before him pointing his barnyard finger of guilt at our DP's.

"You gorgeous blithering idiot, do you know what you've done?" I kept my voice low and casual as if I were saying "Fine haul you've got there, Cap," so the DP's would not know what I thought of my great American Army at that moment.

"If that's not Red Cross parcel stuff..."

"I *gave* it to them. Gave it, do you understand? Christmas present with permission of higher levels. Every single inhabitant got a box with nine items in it, even the nursing babes." I was intoning it soft and low like a lesson learned in endless repetition. I felt no mercy for what was happening to his Caesar's countenance. "Chocolate for the women, cigarettes for the men, distribution by gender with tea, coffee, sugar, biscuits, raisins and liver paste for all. One hundred and eight thousand Red Cross food items were delivered into this camp over the week end, by me, permission from higher echelons. Authorized. Carried out of Supply Area by the DP's themselves because Army couldn't afford to give us any extra gas. Naturally *not,* with this great secret zone-wide blowout in view. *Tally-ho!*"

He was talking into his field phone, a voice out of a central brain talking directly into the earphones of the jeep patrols that controlled sections of blockhouses and the raid squads working through their steamy gray interiors, stopping not quite in mid-air but one at a time from house to house and room to room the efficient khaki-clad arms that reached toward festive tables where sometimes whole villages had got together to pool their Christmas presents, stacking up the shiny tins and pictorial biscuit boxes (even after they had been emptied) just so they could sit around and look a little longer at the produce of Providence and try to imagine what that land must be like which had enough to spare to be able to turn hundreds of rooms across the sea into little grocery stores that certainly would have made the eyes of shopkeeper Jerzszy Tomezewski back home in Horodno bulge with unbelief. And even when it was not a whole village but just a family of ten or fifteen, counting like a Pole the close blood of uncles and cousins, the displays were enough to draw a startled "Holy Smoke!" from the door-rapping troopers, who had always heard that the DP's were smart operators but had never dreamed they were *that* smart, boy oh boy, stealing the stuff right out from under

that bunch of bleeding-hearts called *OON-RAH,* who should never have been given control of the camps in the first place.
You mean the Cap says it's OK?
You mean we lay off the Red Cross stuff?
SNAFU?

It took a lot of talking to slow the thing down, stop it finally, all except the triumphant patrols en route to the courtroom with most of the big shots of the Polish committee and all of the cigarettes we had given to Tak Tak Schön for a New Year distribution to organizations like Former Prisoners of Concentration Camps, the theater groups Stara Banda and Nowy Kacik, and all the choral societies that would be singing unstintingly in hospitals, churches and clubrooms straight through until Epiphany.

The Polish committee arrived in the court just as the captain dropped the field phone back on its hook. Under heavy guard they marched in with senatorial dignity, clad in the caracul turbans and sable-collared greatcoats which they had somehow managed to preserve from moths and Nazis since their abrupt removal from Poland back in '39, and they took their places one by one along the wall, staring at the captain with pale outraged faces. An accompanying lieutenant saluted sharply and spun around to survey the line of patrols staggering in with crates of American cigarettes all neatly packed in the Red Cross boxes, three hundred and sixty-five packages to a carton, exactly as the little scout hands had patted them in to make a top row that came flush with the top of the box.

The captain looked at me once, his face saying plainly, Explain *this* away if you can, my friend, but he said nothing while the boxes were being checked off against the lieutenant's seizure list, watching the scene with the reverential awe generally accorded to bank tellers when they check off bundles of greenbacks, and I thought I would give him a little more time, before I spoke, to complete the TWX I knew he was composing to flash over military wires reporting results of Tally-ho in Wildflecken: AT FIFTEEN HOURS TWENTY-ONE MINUTES PATROLS SEIZED CENTRAL SOURCE US ZONE CIGARETTE BLACK

MARKET STOP ENTIRE POLISH COMMITTEE UNDER ARREST STOP SITUATION WELL IN HAND STOP.

I wondered what Marcel was doing in the prisoners' line-up crushed among the troopers by the door, trying to signal me over the heads of the crowd. Had the raiders picked him up too, mistaking his Belgian army battle jacket and odd baggy pants for one of those quaint khaki outfits tailored from U.S. Army blankets which the DP's were arrested for cutting up and wearing? I expected anything, anything... except what he told me when he had worked his way near enough so I could hear his breathless French.

The German stationmaster, he said, had just telephoned that a thirty-five-car transport bearing one thousand displaced persons had left Brückenau fifteen minutes ago and was due in Wildflecken within the hour. *Ja, bestimmt!*

"Marcel, it's not possible, not possible!" But I knew of course that it was possible, that it was exactly the sort of thing one could expect in Wildflecken with the camp under martial law and every person essential for reception of a transport there before the eyes under arrest — Tak Tak, the Polish quartermaster who assigned space to newcomers, the warehousemen needed to deal out a thousand rations in a hurry and most of Marcel's drivers.

I threw away the beautiful lines I had prepared for the captain. I just said, "Tak Tak... the Polish committee president. He has tally-out signed by our Supply for all those cigarettes. New Year's present to special organizations. Five packs per member. Check his nominal rolls. Count the cigarettes. They'll come out exact, you'll see."

Then I picked up the field phone and handed it to him.

"But before you start checking, would you mind please informing your Army of Occupation that a thousand new DP's are steaming up from Brückenau right now and will begin coming into this camp within an hour, all with identity cards stamped *Passau?* Tell them it's not an illegal infiltration. Just a normal official transfer from Austrian Zone which the masterminds forgot to call off on Tally-ho day."

I fled to find the team. I called Londa from the pass violators' court and left the Countess in charge. Marcel swore he could get a fleet of trucks gassed up and in the station. I found our French warehouseman alone among barrels of flour and lard but willing to try to weigh out one thousand rations and deliver to the camp kitchens. The medical captain, our only team member in a uniform the Army understood, was using his rank to keep patrols out of his Contagious Diseases hospital and Chouka was in her hospital hissing *"TB! Infecte!"* at every uniform approaching her door. I rescued the Canadian nurse from a crowd of weeping women big with child who had flocked to her Maternity to report that their layettes had been confiscated, the clean new yardages of diaper materials she had recently handed out. Yard goods was the folding money of the German black market that winter and *Jeez, how come these Polacks got all this brand-new dry goods salted away for their next tradin' trip to town, huh?*

It takes a long time for the better parts of two Army divisions to fold up their tents and steal away, but they were already working at it when we rode down the hill toward the station. The Signal Corps boys were rolling up the miles of field phone wire that had knit together like a nervous system remote corners of the camp that had never before been in instantaneous contact with its boisterous body around the main square but always a safe fifteen-minute foot journey distant. We saw a sway-backed horse and three goats tethered before Pierre's headquarters offices and two sentinels methodically emptying bottles of confiscated schnapps on bushes that would never bloom again.

We looked so queer huddled together on the immense railroad platform, a handful of broken reeds, a scant half dozen officers where customarily there was a whole trained circus of Polish workers crowding the cobbled stage, yelling orders and countermanding them, shaking sheaves of papers in each others' faces — the DDT dusting squads savagely reminding the billeting officials and truck drivers that they came first in the big act building up, and everybody getting so excited at the prospect of welcoming another group of one's countrymen that sometimes the police had to step in and try to calm things with piercing shouts to which the crowd would respond as if the calliopes had started up.

We stood in the middle of the long loading platform just about where the seventeenth car would stop. We had all reacted automatically to the icy white solitude surrounding us and had centered ourselves, trying to make ourselves look like a crowd so the incoming Poles would not be frightened and think they had arrived in a Siberian wasteland bleak and unpopulated.

We felt no anxiety about unloading a transport of one thousand human souls all alone. We simply waited for it. The actions to be performed, the instantaneous decisions to be made, had long since become reflexes and there was not a contingency that could arise which we had not met before a hundred, a thousand times. It was as if the transports had somehow got into our blood stream, established themselves there like a new hormone which, at the proper moment, we could count upon to send the right messages through our weary bodies, telling the motionless muscles what to do.

Nobody except Londa glanced backward at the pine-clad hill concealing a camp city so muted in the silence of fear and confusion that you would have thought only the foxes walked there. If you did not look that way, you did not have to begin to think of the colossal clean-up job to be done after Army would roll out leaving neatly segregated mountains of goods to be redistributed and stacks of wallet-worn, only slightly illegible, identity cards to be rewritten and reissued. Londa stared toward the camp saying "Bloody, *bloody...*" but with all fury drained from her voice so that she might have been remarking conversationally the reddish glow which a sinking sun threw over the patches of snow visible between black pines.

The rest of us measured the remaining daylight against the steam whistle sounding up the valley. We knew we had eleven cars of daylight left and that the other twenty-four cars would have to be unloaded in the dark.

~ 9 ~

The DP world turned into an Alice-in-Wonderland world in 1946. Afterwards, the entire year seemed to have had the odd quality of a protracted lost week end that was difficult to recall, as if somehow it had dropped from the calendar the way certain vegetative years of childhood disappear from later reckoning. We began the year in innocence, believing it was to be our last with the DP's, believing every fine flowery speech in their behalf which came over our battered radios, mercifully unaware that it would be yet another full year before the first Western democracy would open its doors to our displaced ones (and that one Belgium, still on the continent of Europe, not safely overseas where everyone wanted to go) and that it would not be until the summer of 1948 when the golden doors of "Neuyorke Amerika" would open, cautiously.

Like our DP's, we lived on hope, but unlike them, we had something more to do than sit around and produce babies meanwhile at such a fruitful pace that soon the per capita birth rate of DP-land would exceed that of any other country except possibly China. We hardly had time even to sit down. We were the appointed guardians of a small lopsided corner of earth where things quite definitely were growing queerer and queerer.

Centered in a continent of hunger, Wildflecken rose up before German eyes like a magic mountain made of sugar and Spam, of margarine and jam, bearing forests of cigarettes (four packs per week per worker) and carpeted with vitaminized chocolate bars.

The eyes of a people whose ration in February had been reduced to a daily eighteen hundred calories looked at their former slaves, who were getting twenty-three hundred calories, as if they were wayfarers from some fabulous land, and the staring eyes were bloodless as the winter cabbages dug up out of sod trenches to be the mainstay of the German diet until the next crop season. The German eyes were not dull and apathetic, however; they glinted to the lure of a mountain of food that did not even have a fence around it and it was no trick at all for our Poles to turn Wildflecken into a tourist trap. It was a sort of after New Year sport that broke the monotony of just sitting around waiting for something to happen. The Poles, seigneurs of Wildflecken, would saunter in neighboring towns waiting for some German to mention their camp with interest and someone usually did, very often someone who could speak a little Polish picked up during the Nazi sojourn in Poland. The German was then invited to come up on the train someday and have a look around. He was promised that he would be met at the station and taken on a conducted tour, and he was. He was led into camp over one of the rabbit trails out of sight of the main gate and taken directly to the big open-air trading mart at the top of the camp, where he could not resist stocking up on margarine, chocolate bars and as many cigarettes as his worn briefcase could hold, and our tipped-off DP police always waited patiently until it could hold no more. Then they arrested the German for illegal entry into camp and possession of unauthorized goods and turned him over in style to Military Government for trial. How many ancient grudges were paid off in this bloodless fashion before we caught on to what was going on, we could never surmise. And even after we had caught on, there was nothing we could do about it except wait for the Poles to tire of the sport and invent something else to kill time.

Meanwhile, in a different part of camp, our wild world added a paradise to its curious cosmology. This paradise was the end result of another mass VD examination which Army ordered as part of its annual housecleaning — a painful ordeal for thousands of our self-respecting men and women and just another *divertissement* for some of our tougher souls, who, after having been catalogued, X-rayed, fingerprinted and inoculated so many times before, now offered up their bodies to one more smear test without feeling anything except genial wonder at the myriad manifestations of international relief.

Military Government sent us two German doctors to assist our haggard medical and nursing comrades and penicillin for the cure of gonorrhea cases. The second floor of the Contagious Diseases hospital was set aside for GC ward, and here we incarcerated the positive cases for three days, "provoking" on the second day and making another smear test on the third day, just to be doubly sure. And it was here, while the miracle of penicillin worked its swift cure, that the phenomenon of paradise unfolded slowly. Once again we were laboring so mightily in the vineyard we failed to see what was happening over our heads. We heard the Poles talking about paradise. When a key worker would be absent from his job and we would ask, "Where's Wasyl today?" someone would reply with a grin, *"Im Paradies."*

Then one night our medical captain, making his rounds, ran into the crowd in front of the Contagious Diseases hospital, an immense and joyous crowd shouting hurrahs for the lucky ones *im Paradies* and looking up to the second-floor windows of the GC ward, from which leaned the sojourners in "paradise," shouting back helpful advice on what to do to get sent to such a splendid place where there was nothing to do all day but lie about and eat the special food from the hospital kitchen and if you don't believe that this is luxury compared to what comes out of the camp kitchens, then just take a taste of that, Babushka... and there were buckets on strings being lowered from hospital windows to friends and well-wishers in the street below and here and there a bottle of schnapps going back up on the dangled strings and, said our dumfounded captain when at last he had tottered down to the billets for a good stiff drink of whiskey, under the west wing, where we isolated the female cases, there were accordion troubadours serenading those hussies clustered at the windows taking their bows just like strip-tease queens...

Of course, in this weird wonderland, you could not read any of the signs because all of them were either upside down or going around in circles, none of which ever extended beyond the perimeter of the camp, and so we had no way of knowing that what we were really seeing were the first small rents in the tough fabric of DP morale, the inevitable result of penning up a sturdy people who loved the earth and wanted to put a plow into it, an artistic people who carried in their genes perhaps another Paderewski, another Curie, another Chopin, a long-suffering people finally rescued, relieved, cured of their ailments and fattened up from starvation's skeletons to the shape of men again, but now with no place to go. We misread the signs, we failed to see the rents.

It was as if we were living in a small room with a tremendous and turbulent tapestry, Gothic in grandeur and dense in design, that went around all four walls, the teeming totality of it coming to us with every upward glance, but never the single stitch, the frayed edge, the threadbare spot in the middle of the battle scene. All life was in this tumultuous thing that surrounded us, every imaginable aspect of it from the humorous to the frightening, pulsing, beating and twisting in upon itself because there was no place else for its pent vitality to go except inward and around and around, evolving in its endless arabesques strange blooms like "paradise" and German-baiting and sometimes a pale corpse or two...

On a late March night we stared at the corpses of two of our Polish men which an ambulance brought in out of the shivering white brightness of the snowy slopes that hemmed us in toward the west. One cadaver had its throat slit and was stripped clean of clothes; the other, with only the boots taken off, had a fist-sized gun wound in the left flank. A small sack of khaki caps, such as our camp tailors made from forbidden Army blankets, and a big tin colander, accompanied the bodies. It did not seem strange to us how instantaneously and how naturally we read the evidence of caps and colander, seeing our two young men setting out that morning in the icy gray dawnlight before gate guards were wide awake, to do a bit of trading in those remote German villages hidden in the tar-black woods beyond the white slopes westward, swinging the colander in which they hoped to bring back some kraut and the sack of caps that could not be sold in camp, where no one would risk wearing a piece of Army blanket on the head, laughing probably as they stretched their camp-cramped legs toward the wider places of "outside" and talking doubtless about that comrade who last week had ventured all the way up to the seaport cities in the British Zone and had brought back a briefcase stuffed with smoked herring which he had built up into a small fortune in skillful swapping. Nodding their heads, *Tak tak,* you could do almost as good with a few kilos of kraut, especially when there had not been anything resembling a vegetable for weeks and weeks in the camp.

The captain examined the gun wound and said, "Machine gun or repeating rifle of thirty or thirty-two caliber," and told us women to get away from the ambulance, it was no sight for a woman's eyes.

"Army rifle, Herr Doktor. We saw... ah, the *Schweinehund...*" Kowalski panted, perspired, stuttered and started again. First there had been that German woman in a black sedan who had reported the night before to his gate guard that there was blood in the snow over there by Langenleiten and she sped away before his *Dummkopf* guard could get her name or car number. He and his men went forth and found the blood, then the bodies, then the boot tracks leading off from where this one lay, the bootless one. It was easy to follow the tracks because they were from Polish boots that have their hobnails driven in in a certain pattern. The hobnail tracks went about three kilometers into the forest and there his men came upon a bunker like those in hillside caves where Germans sometimes store root vegetables or wine, only in this deserted place such a bunker could not have been logical. There were here many prints trampled in the snow and still the faint studding of the Polish hobnails. And it was just then that a German came out of the bunker firing point-blank with a *prima* Army rifle. Kowalski's men fired back and then five more Germans sprang from the ground, shooting, so they fled, our DP police, but not before they had seen on their attackers those black jackets with the stiff-braided military cuffs...

Rumors of SS regroupings had been circulating for quite some time all over Germany in the talk of the Occupation people, but our DP's, cloistered in their camps, had not yet seemed aware of this potential threat and had not added it to the processional bogeymen that stalked their dreams led by the Russian Bear. Now we knew, no matter how solemnly Kowalski swore to Pierre with his hand over his thumping heart that not a word, not a whisper of this would reach the camp, that the phantom SS man would now take his place in the bogeylore of Wildflecken.

We had not completed our formal report of the unsolved double murder before the story was all over the camp and spectral SS men in the dreaded black tunics were seen creeping through our dark encircling forests, peering with red eyes of hate at the Poles moving about in a camp that had once belonged to them, had in fact been built exclusively to house them in high lonely grandeur away from the common herd while they coached themselves to conquer the world.

Anxiety queued up at our office door while Pierre and I put the finishing touches to another "incident report" which, like all preceding ones, read like another chapter (complete this time with mystery woman, black sedan and stiff white bodies of two young bachelors) in the Nick Carter serial which we supposed H.Q. thought we were writing to relieve the tedium of our days. We seldom had a reply on our piecemeal production and, in time, we came to believe that the thumbtack representing Wildflecken on some central headquarters map had probably dropped out and been carried away on the sole of someone's shoe.

While the imaginary SS men roamed our woods, we waited for the first thaw in a period of comparative quiet because very few DP's wanted to leave camp. Then Churchill spoke from Fulton, Missouri, and everybody wanted to leave camp at once and our population packed its bags while Stalin's reply lashed back over Radio Moscow, to which camp sets were continuously tuned, and there was such a vibration of nerves and fear that even we began staring toward the east at the bald white peak called Wasserkuppe which marked the boundary between our U.S. Zone and the Russian Zone. It was barely twenty miles distant as the crow flies. We knew no more than our DP's but we had to act as if we did. We wore masks of pretense until our faces were paralyzed with the continuing effort. We could not risk removal of our masks even in the billets, where our Polish housemaids watched our faces and, we suspected, kept track of our duffel bags and suitcases stored in the attics to see if any of us were packing too.

The Poles sat on their packed bags and waited to be evacuated from Wildflecken and a little Polish man stood before Pierre's desk crying and hysterical and babbling that his wife could not be moved because she was too ill and would we give an ambulance to transport her? *Move? Move to where?* we shouted from behind our masks. Where those four hundred trucks lined up outside the main gate were going, toward the west, toward the west. And there were no trucks at the gate. There were only the empty cobbled road and the vacant train tracks beyond but no Pole even bothered to go down and see for himself because this was the rumor, this was believed.

A delegation of camp leaders — Tak Tak, the schoolteachers, the priests — came in and said what can we do to stop the panic and is Wildflecken going to close? These were serious people, the real leaders of our troubled flock, our intelligentsia. They were not the little people who could be soothed by a "There, there, don't be afraid, there's nothing, but really nothing, out there at all."

"We must have something specific to take back to the camp, Herr Direktor." Tak Tak spread his hands on his knees and looked straight at Pierre, his calm practical merchant's face waiting for the goods to be named.

"Rumors, rumors, Mr. President," said Pierre. "Not to our knowledge will this camp be evacuated."

"Facts I need," said Tak Tak. "There is a mass meeting. The people wait. You must send us back with facts. Otherwise — " he lifted his spread hands and signed surrender with them in the air — "we cannot be responsible."

The telephone rang and Pierre reached for it. We could all hear the fuzzy sounds of a long-distance voice. The *deus ex machina* of wonderland, of course. I knew by Pierre's relieved expression that he was listening to the fact that would calm the hysteria. "Yes, yes, I have got it. On March twenty-seventh at eleven hours..." Pierre hung up and gave the goods to the waiting merchant.

"Now go back to your people," he said, "and ask them if Army would be sending us one thousand more Poles if Wildflecken were considered a danger spot. One thousand newcomers. Start the machinery to receive them in three days' time."

The machinery started, the people unpacked their bags, tension went from the atmosphere and we could take off our masks. And all that this unconscious rehearsal for the Berlin airlift cost us was two suicides from fear and three miscarriages in women who had shoved too much heavy luggage around.

I could not wait to get aboard the first transport out to Poland that year, as if I knew even then in its still hopeful and heartbreakingly beautiful spring that the bickering and bargaining disunited Western world would be able to offer no other solution, no other place to go, except eastward to Poland. We had been told that we could accompany the transports if we wished. It was as voluntary for UNRRA officers as it was for the DP's. I jumped at the opportunity. If I could bring back even the smallest shred of encouragement, I said to Pierre, wouldn't that at least be something?

"Ma pauvre petite fleur bleue," said Pierre, looking at me as if I were actually a little blue flower, tender and believing in the spring.

Besides, I went on to my winning point, it might even encourage signatures on the repatriation list if the camp knew that one of its own officers would accompany the first transport of the year.

The first list of voluntary repatriants totaled eighty-nine. The Polish committee in a body brought the single page of names to Pierre.

"Is this all?" Pierre asked, trying to imagine himself telephoning that total to the Army that considered one thousand persons a good economical load for a transport.

"There will be one more, Herr Direktor." Tak Tak read his spread hands thoughtfully. "My name will be on that list."

"Is this known in the camp?"

"Tak tak."

"And it does not encourage more?"

"Not after what happened ten days ago. That... that conversation between Churchill and Stalin," Tak Tak explained patiently as if we had not been in the camp at the time, "it did not fly over our heads in the air waves between two continents. Each word went through our bodies first, then onwards, only *then* onwards. Also, Herr Direktor, the camp knows I have nothing more to lose." Only in the faces of his committee comrades could you see in quick compassionate remembering the shadow of his personal sorrow, the blitz victims he had buried in Poland so many years ago, his wife and two sons. Tak Tak's face was steady and stern as a symbol representing total loss.

"If the camp knew perhaps that an UNRRA officer would go along also, do you think that might help?" Pierre looked at me, his skeptic's eyes saying, You win, against his will. "Our deputy director has applied for permission to accompany the transport."

"This may achieve something." Tak Tak stood up and bowed to me. "If you will permit, we will place a notice in the camp newspaper."

Four days later I rode out of Wildflecken in a boxcar bound for Poland, with two hundred and twenty repatriants, one lieutenant and eleven GI guards and two large American flags tacked on both sides of the military escort car. With a French nurse from another camp in Germany, I rode in what was called the "hospital car" because a big red cross outlined in white was still visible on its scarred and scaly exterior.

Ignatz ran beside the "hospital car" until the end of the cobbled platform and then he released my hand and waved me off with tears of woe streaming down his face and a *Dowidzenia* so choked and fearful that it sounded like farewell forever.

~ 10 ~

Ten days in a boxcar riding across Central Europe in the spring spoils you for any other kind of travel, especially if you have a little hobo blood in your veins. You sit on the swept floor with your legs hanging out on whichever side the April sun is shining, rolling along quite slowly just four feet above fields of young grain and clover which you can smell as intimately as if you were out there face down on the sap-sweet earth. You rock along and wait for the incurves to come so you can lean out and wave to friends in the forward and the following cars and maybe point with excitement at a loping hare or a birch grove hazy pink in early bud. And everyone watches the engine wheezing and huffing at the head of the clanking linked cars, manufacturing hot water for a shave or a wash-up, which the engineer will spigot off into your bucket for the price of a few cigarettes at the next stop.

The next stop could be anywhere and at any hour... but it was a thing to be used when it came. The cities and towns of Germany and Czechoslovakia were just freight yards to us — Nürnberg, Schwandorf, Furth im Wald; then Domazlice, Pilsen and Prague. We slid into their sooty gray sidings that looked exactly alike and immediately set up housekeeping on their narrow cinder paths between tracks, doing all the things that could not be accomplished while we were shaking along in seventeen boxcars with no communication between. Toward the supply car from each of the other cars came blankets upheld at the corners by laughing Poles while the food for the next lap of the journey was tossed into them.

Toward our hospital car came the Irish lieutenant, our train commander, to give a hand to Claudette, the French nurse, as she climbed down with a medical kit of aspirin and soda bicarbonate tablets, bandages, iodine and laxatives, and to follow her staring at her red hair as if it were a sunrise, as she made her "home visits" down the string of boxcars. And at every stop, I had to see Babchia first because I too had lost my heart — to an eighty-five-year-old granny who rode in car 12 with nineteen boisterous bachelors, going home all alone to Poland, not to die, but to seek the last two remaining of her fourteen sons, who someone had said were alive in Cracow.

On each cinder path of each freight yard where we stopped, we left the rich debris of the American repatriation train — cigarette ends and sardine cans with still a spoonful of olive oil clinging in their corners, heels of bread and biscuit tins of clean useful British tin; and then our engine returned, having taken on its drink of water or load of coal, and pulled us away from the mess we had made. We watched the German urchins scurrying in to clean it up as we rolled out singing to the next stop on a similar cinder path.

Perhaps it was the singing that turned Claudette, the Irish lieutenant and me into DP's going home to Poland. There was nearly continuous singing, not from the whole train at once but from this car or from that one, ahead or behind, so that always you heard above the metallic grind of high iron wheels on rails the soughing echo of impromptu choral groups and on the incurves you could often see which car was singing. And when, on the third day, we came into Czechoslovakia and saw no bogeymen in Russian greatcoats with the stiff horizontal epaulets, and had no radios, cameras or musical instruments confiscated at the border crossing point, the singing soared above the sound of iron on iron and even Tak Tak Schön, leaning, swaying and waving from the rear car, almost smiled. We all went slightly crazy in Czechoslovakia, it was so beautiful that spring.

I watched the beginning of it in Domazlice as we pulled into our first Czech city at six o'clock on an April morning. We pulled in between strings of sealed boxcars identical with all the others we had slept between or lived our stopover hours among, and the cinder paths looked the same as all those of Germany which we had despoiled and rolled away from... but there was something different in the air. You felt at once that you were out of Germany, out of that sad static land of ruins and DP camps. Most of our Poles were up. The men leaped from the boxcars even before we ground to a halt and they propped their shaving mirrors on the ladderlike iron steps, tilting them to catch the first slant rays of rising sun. A regular bucket brigade visited the hissing engine before it got away to cool its boilers with another long drink at the water tower. The women stood in the wide-flung doors of the cars and poured the water down on their men's bared backs and there was such a scrubbing and shaving and bathing going on along the cinder path, you would have thought it was mass preparation for a lovers' tryst. Then smoke started curling out from boxcar chimneys. We had time to boil our coffee water, heat the baby bottles and prepare thin gruel for children and old folks while the train stood still in the sooty freight yards.

Then we pulled out into a land where people were smiling, where golden pheasants were running across newly sprouted grainfields and where hares the size of fox terriers sat in unscared circles near where Czech farmers guided plows behind horses... *Pferde! Pferde!...* not cow-drawn as in Germany but horse-drawn as plows should be. Once, a beautiful Czech peasant woman stood out bold atop a rail embankment blue with wild violets and when she called to the Poles, *"Wohin gehen Sie?"* you were not sure that you too had not joined in their glad proud call-back... *"Nachhause... nach Heim!"* We're going home!

In Pilsen the trading began and it was so good to see the Poles acting like millionaires with their special repatriation ration of cigarettes that you did not think how long it must have been since tobacco was last seen in Czechoslovakia. The Czech rail-yard men came down the tracks with imitation leather briefcases under their arms. They brought Czech brandy, harmonicas, costume jewelry, silk bloomers and bangle bracelets with enameled flags of all Allied nations, including Russia (which killed sales to our Poles), and our GI's were buying as feverishly as the repatriants, haggling over rings set with great hunks of red glass and ignoring the heirloom brooches of genuine garnet, while the lieutenant hollered at all of us not to buy the plum brandy yet, it would drop from five packs of cigarettes the bottle to two packs, just before departure time.

I walked down as always to Babchia's car. Her young men had fixed a seat for her in the sun at the car door, a smooth round log of firewood which they had upended like a low stool, and there she sat, an aged and delicate queen mother in her black ribbed-velvet bodice with small bright flowers printed on it and her spotlessly clean apron smoothed down over her full woven wool skirt. Her incredibly thin, nearly transparent hands were folded quietly in her aproned lap but her clear blue eyes, set deep in the crinkled face, were shiny with cunning as they flashed over the furious trading scene. As I was putting a PX mint patty in her folded hands, she cackled with stern and sudden vigor *"Nie nie!"* to an overeager Pole and stopped a too-easy sale instantly.

Plum brandy whetted the singing throats from Pilsen onward and now in the stops it was impossible for us merely to look in each car door as we made our rounds with medicines, candy and condensed milk. We had to climb into each breast-high boxcar and have a nip from this bottle or from that one, or listen to the air Wasyl had already learned on his new harmonica, or simply sit there and smile agreement on how fine all this was. If perchance we stood below and shook our heads — *Nie nie,* no more strength left to climb into another car — the men leaned down and lifted us bodily up into it with our bulging knapsack or medical kit flying along behind us through the air. And very often there we were sitting when the train pulled out, toasting Poland, Kosciusko, Pulaski or Paderewski while the freight yards of Prague, Pardubice, Česká Třebová or Ústí nad Orlicí slipped away past the open door.

As we came closer to the Polish frontier, I forgot everything I had ever thought or felt about repatriation. It was not the thirty-five per cent Czech brandy that was adding up sip by sip. It was the unexpected joyous elation of our Poles lifting higher and sharper with each kilometer traversed, which caught me in its keen contagion and made the gray doubts of Wildflecken seem a dim distorted memory.

The last night in Czechoslovakia, I was caught in Babchia's car. The withered little granny was sitting erect on her bedding roll near the stove, surrounded by the men of her car, who had copied my ardor for her and were serving her the strong tea and soft pap-food I had ordered. They arranged a box for me beside Babchia so I could sit with my arm around her fragile waist and admire close up the handsome flowered head shawl she had put on for her entry into Poland. The train pulled out so quietly, I was unaware we were moving until I saw a semaphore go by. The men began to sing almost at once. The male voices lifted strongly above the iron clatter and presently you did not hear the train at all, only the folk songs of Poland one after another, until the vibration in that car rose so high you felt it might almost be dangerous for an old lady of eighty-five years. Alternately she was weeping and laughing with the songs, swinging her head and tapping her foot, looking proudly through the candlelight at her people who had not forgotten in their long exile the words, gestures and intonations of their country's oldest chants. Sometimes when they paused after a song, bringing their shining faces closer to the candles and thinking what next to sing, Babchia called the tune in a quavering but authoritative voice, with a foxy glint in her clear blue eyes, and I knew by the way her thin hand tightened in mine that she was calling a tune which only their grandmothers could have taught them... and when they sang that one through for her, she would embrace them with tears streaming down her face and I feared she might evaporate within the circle of my arm, so great was her emotion. Once I fished around in the deep pocket under her apron where she hoarded the chocolate I brought, and I extracted a Hershey bar and made her eat a piece of it for strength to bear her up in her joy.

New candles were thrust upon the stumps of burned ones. At intervals the small iron door of the stove was opened for stoking and a red light glittered momentarily on the cracked cups and small glasses placed on a box in our midst, holding the garnet liquor of plums. Late in the night in a brief halt, I saw the face of the lieutenant peering into the car and I called to him saying, "Come in here, come see what you're *really* guarding and taking home to Poland," and then he was there with us, crouched on the other side of Babchia with his arm around her, riding with us for a way and listening to the men sing.

How could you have heard above that virile uplift of joyous home-going voices the creaky rustle of an iron curtain swaying insidiously westward? How could you have guessed that what you were really taking in was the haunting material for heartbreak? Your only thought then was, How beautiful are people going home.

We ordered our repatriants to remain in their own cars when we came into Ostrava, the last Czech town, the border control point. A Czech agent came to count each car's population against our nominal roll. The cars fell quiet at his approach until it was seen that the uniform he wore was the familiar dark green of the railroad company and that the military accouterments upon it — belt, cross straps and cap visor — were only of comic opera patent leather. Then, as the roll was read off, the answering *Tak* came firm and fearless from inside each car whether in a man's or a woman's or a child's voice. No baggage was touched. The dapper agent did not even put his head inside the cars to look at the mountainous piles stacked in corners. The tongue-twister Polish names took more than three hours to call off. It was after sunset when at last we pulled away.

The distance between Ostrava and Zebrydowice, the first village inside Poland, was measured in a few velvety grainfields, a lane of weeping willows just coming into leaf and a bridge under construction over a deep river channel. The train stopped on the skeletal bridge. Our young men swarmed from the cars like monkeys and began coming down the perilous trestle to our hospital car. They stood straddle on railroad ties laid across space crying "That's Poland! Poland!" nearly losing their balance as they pointed forward while we screamed at them to get back in their cars, get back in their cars. My God! To be killed within a stone's throw of the homeland. The train started with a jerk which threw Claudette and me back into our car and spared us having to watch the Poles leaping through the air to catch at the high iron ladders of the passing cars.

We glided into Zebrydowice, a country village among clover fields, with a small gay station featuring a flag-decked pavilion of the P.U.R. (Polish Committee of Repatriation), posters of bold fine design saying *Welcome to Poland — We will all work together* and a loud-speaker giving off dance music.

At first the Poles were shy in their own land. They got down from their boxcars and stood in groups under the station's arc lights, looking toward the P.U.R. pavilion a bit critically as if they had seen better than that where they came from. A few moved toward the bulletin boards to read the Warsaw newspapers tacked up there. Then, someone discovered that free coffee was being dispensed from the station café and our diffident Poles turned suddenly into hosts at home in their own land, with first thought for us, the visitors there. They brought us cups of it to drink and would not take no for an answer. The liquid was made from some kind of roasted grain, slightly sugared, but it was coffee-brown and the cups all had handles and this was Poland, wasn't it, a country to drink to if ever there was one. White cups were carried eagerly to boxcars to those who had not yet descended. Cup rims clinked together. *Dobre, dobre,* said our Poles over and over, a soft word, the word for good, referring at first to the imitation coffee upheld in the white cups, then expanding to include everything there before the eyes — the flag-bright pavilion, the busy bulletin boards, the heroic posters and the wide Polish night out beyond where the smell of clover came from.

Babchia sat on her upended stove log at the edge of her car's doorway with her handsome shawl draped carefully over head and shoulders and there was an arc light just before that car so she looked like the central figure set up on a small stage. No one had to suggest to the dramatic-minded Poles that that was the place to gather for the singing of the national anthem.

They gathered slowly until there was a small crowd before the door, then everyone came in quickly to see what was going on around car 12. A woman's clear high soprano led them off. Our lieutenant and his GI's whipped off their hats and stood at attention. I knew that Polish anthem as well as my own "Star-Spangled Banner," but I had never heard it sung like that, by two hundred and twenty repatriants with their feet on home soil for the first time in seven years. It was a relief when it was over and everyone began to cry frankly and openly. Then the semicircle of repatriated humanity around Babchia's car wound arms about each other's shoulders and made a kind of fan stemming out from her tapping toe, a living fan all of one piece that swayed to the tempo of new songs sung, quickening to martial airs, slowing to thanksgiving hymns and undulating gently like wheat in the wind to old folk songs full of peace and plenty.

That was the last time we really saw our DP repatriants, although we were going to be with them for several hours the next morning in Dziedzice when we would sign them over to P.U.R., watch them get registered and photographed, share their interest in the money exchange that gave one Polish zloty for one Allied mark and their excitement at the discovery that one American cigarette could be sold in Poland for six zlotys or sixty cents, and, at last, take photographs of some of the families climbing into second-class railway carriages with Warsaw, Katowice or Cracow printed clearly on the plaque affixed to the side of the car. But that next morning they would no longer be DP's or repatriants belonging to us. They would all be Polish citizens then.

Claudette, the lieutenant and I stood for a while at the edge of the swaying singing crowd. The repatriants were woven so tightly together with interlocking arms that the whole fan-shaped mass moved as one horizontally back and forth, closing out from their compact unity everything that did not belong to that high moment of homecoming realized — even their own people, the Polish station agent and café waitresses, who had never left the land but who stood near us staring into the arc light as if for the first time they were really seeing Poland. Then the lieutenant took one of us on each arm and walked us up to his command car where the plum brandy waited.

"Morale was high is how you write *that* up in your report," he said at last. "Easy. Just three words..."

That was the way it was in the Easter month of April 1946. Smooth and easy, every mile between Germany and Poland recorded in song and never a backward glance once the first frontier was crossed safely. I would have said it was too good to be true if I had not personally experienced every memorable mile of it. Back in Wildflecken the DP's said, *Look she's returned, she actually escaped and got out,* and looked at me as Ignatz looked at the bottle of Polish vodka I had bought for him in Dziedzice, turning it round and round in his hand, bewildered by the bright solid proof I had presented. But the faces that gazed long and longingly at the snapshots I had mounted on the repatriation bulletin board were filled with homesickness and I believed that it would take only one or two more successful transports to dissipate the fear and foreboding that lay over the camp like a gray spell. I even began counting ahead, I was flying so high, I was so sure. I raised the numbers for each successive transport until we would arrive at the good round economical figure of one thousand repatriants per week. "And from then on," I said to Pierre, "you can count it out on your knuckles. In ten weeks we will have this problem licked. Wildflecken can be given back to the Indians, or to the regrouped SS."

My elation lasted exactly ten days, the time it took Chouka to accompany the second transport to Poland and to return with a report of how Czechoslovakia looked just after the big May Day celebrations, while the hammer-and-sickle flags were still flying from public buildings side by side with the Czech flags. And the two carefully selected DP observers from our camp, whom Army had authorized to go into Poland with her and return to Germany to tell all they had seen and heard, brought back tales of a raid of partisans into Dziedzice the day before they arrived and of a rounding up of all suspected Communists in that border town — which was probably why, Chouka said, nobody in the town would talk above a whisper and *Ma foi!* she thought she had run into a laryngitis epidemic. But it was not until Chouka had developed and duly mounted her photographs for public viewing that the whole camp reacted as a single outraged being. One of her practical documentary shots showed a post-box on a Dziedzice street corner with the customary (so we thought) Polish eagle embossed on its front. The DP's pointed in shock at their national symbol: the traditional white eagle of Poland had no crown. *Tak tak,* said the DP observers, the provisional government had removed all the crowns from the great white eagle of Poland. Wildflecken went into mourning and a spate of crowned eagles issued from our handicraft shops, embroidered on silk, cut from tin, sculptured in wood, while we received a military inspection to inquire why repatriation had dropped off to a mere trickle. It was just like old times. We were almost back where we had started, in the dead static of no place to go.

Londa accompanied the third transport out, which had to be hooked up to one from another camp in Germany because it was too small to merit a locomotive all to itself. She left Wildflecken fuming, "Oh, the stupid, *stupid* fools!" and threatening to jump channels to contact the provisional government personally to tell them what their idiotic crown-removing gesture was costing them in repatriable manpower — "as if you could remove the stripes from the Union Jack or the stars from the American flag." But she had no time for that when she was in Poland. She spent her day-long stopover in the office of the chief of police trying to bail from a Polish jail her two female DP observers, who had been arrested at the first show window where they had paused to copy prices of foodstuffs on display, for the encouragement of future repatriation. And, when they returned to Germany, it was an even tossup which story frightened the Wildflecken housewives the most — four hundred zlotys for one kilo of fat in Poland or the alleged presence of a Russian officer in the town's jail who had spent the day grilling our two welfare observer ladies.

There was a lull in repatriation after that. It lasted for a whole month while the June rains fell and the world outside our static camp tried to think what to do to get those DP's to go somewhere. Ignatz became a father again, this time of the son he so deserved; he seemed to be the only completely happy individual in the entire camp. Tempers on the team flared and depression caught at the strongest. We had twenty-four members now, but no one looked new or different. There was a sameness to all the faces watching over those masses of displaced persons as if constant exposure to human woe had made some radical change in the psyche.

The DP's we took off incoming transports began to look the same, too, but in a different way. Their universal expression was of weariness and despair. The Army was moving them around again, shifting groups from camp to camp, uprooting them as soon as they had tacked up a private-room partition or strung a light bulb, giving them no chance to create a temporary home, in the hopes that maybe they might begin thinking of their real home in Poland and go there, if for no other reason than for the peace of staying put. It looked like a cruel and senseless scheme to break the deadlock, but no voice outside our tight and teeming Occupation world spoke up with a better solution or, for that matter, with any mention at all of the displaced — as if, at war's end, all that dreary and embarrassing refugee business had ended too, swept as cleanly from the record as the tears and tremolos of the Dachau discoveries had vanished from newspaper headlines.

We divided our team into two separate teams so we could give day and night service to our incoming transports from Hanau, Mannheim, Darmstadt, Esslingen, Karlsruhe, Kassel, Coburg, Wetzlar, Aschaffenburg, Würzburg, Ansbach, Wiesbaden, from every DP camp in the U.S. Zone which contained Poles who were settling in too comfortably. *Keep them moving* was the watchword and the dead-beat "irrepatriables" flowed into Wildflecken until every blockhouse was filled to its attic rafters and the basement barnyards blossomed with light bulbs strung from stall to stall where hardy homesteaders were housekeeping because now there was no other living space left in the camp. And one day in August I knocked over a great bunch of lavender autumn crocus which Ignatz had put on my desk when I read my copy of Supply's weekly ration requisition and learned that we had twenty thousand DP's again.

It looked as if we were back exactly where we had started a year ago. But there was to be one last act in the mass drama of Polish repatriation before the iron curtain would swing out to include Poland in the list of lost lands to which only people with special reasons would return voluntarily. We could not know, of course, that we were working against curtain-time as we set the scene for that last peculiar act, or that that curtain-time had the definite date of January 19, 1947, when the Yalta-promised free elections would take place in Poland... and turn out to be as rigged as any plebiscite ever was in any totalitarian land. All we knew was that we still had some fine fall months left for boxcar travel and that now the policymakers were going to bait our DP's to go home with a sixty-day ration of food offered to every repatriant who returned to Poland before the end of '46.

We set the scene for that last act on a night in September while Wildflecken was sleeping. We went forth with flashlights and paste pots and rolls of billboard material which a special courier from higher levels had delivered to us. When our DP's awakened next morning, they found their camp city plastered with a magnificent "Proclamation Addressed to All Poles in Germany" from the President of the Minister's Council in Warsaw, promising friendly reception to the brothers in exile, reconstruction jobs in all walks of life, free transport by P.U.R. inside Poland and a two-month reserve of food to be distributed free by UNRRA to each repatriant immediately upon his arrival in Stettin or Dziedzice. Maps of Poland and a special letter from General McNarney, telling the Poles that there was not much hope for resettlement elsewhere than in Poland, flanked the proclamations.

In the big general meeting place of the camp canteen we set up a permanent preview of the sixty-day food ration, which amounted to some ninety-four pounds of food per person — flour, dried peas, rolled oats, salt, evaporated milk, canned fish and a small mountain of lard. Ignatz worked with me on the visual display, giving it art touches like slashing the sack of flour and spilling a little on the table so everyone could see it was fine white American flour and not the dingy tan mixture of German rye used in the camp's bakery, carving a floral design on the lard and stacking the tinned goods in perilous pyramids. And this was only the handout in miniature, the food for a single person. On another table longer and stronger we set up what a family of four would receive, three hundred and seventy-six pounds of food, and the mound of lard in this display had enough mass to permit sculpture of the white eagle of Poland on its front surface.

"This one," said Ignatz, tooling spread claws on his fatty white eagle, "one could trade for a horse, for some acres, even for a house *vielleicht!*" But not I, said his face of habitual renunciation, not I in my expropriated village on the Russian side of the River Bug; I cannot be bought with food. He stepped back and squinted professionally at his eagle. Then he wiped his knife and swiftly cut a crown over its proud profiled head.

All day long the Poles filed past the food displays. The awestruck processional continued for weeks and weeks until the sculptured lard had been whittled away by scooping fingers, until the spilled flour disappeared handful by handful, until the stacked tinned goods had no more flying buttresses to the rear as Ignatz had built them in to support the steep sheen of the front turrets.

By October the homebound movement was in full swing again. Bigwigs from Army and from our own H.Q. swarmed the camp "to see how the thing worked." They congratulated us and made us proud of the speed of our repatriation machinery, which could process eight hundred Poles and load a string of boxcars every three or four days, with a numbered card in the hand of every repatriant entitling him to draw that wonder-working sixty-day food ration as soon as he arrived in Poland.

The crescendo of outgoing transports caught us up, swept us, with braying brass bands and crashing of boxcars switching in and slamming out, back into the old familiar frenzy of continual movement with no time for thought or feeling.

Gradually we forgot the secret shame we had felt when we had first stood beside the free food displays and had watched our DP's stare at the terrible fascination of the bait, thrashing, twisting and turning before they took the hook.

~ 11 ~

The year 1947 was going to be the despair year for our DP's, their year of door-watching with all eyes focused on the tight-shut portals of the United States while iron curtains clanked ominously all around, in Poland, Yugoslavia and Czechoslovakia, and History gave them her advance releases on coming events, using humans instead of newsprint to tell the startling stories. There was just one electric flash of hope when a sort of trial balloon called the Truman Doctrine began to operate, permitting a few extremely "compassionate cases" to enter the States. But only one from our great camp had enough pressure and power working for her on the other side to get her across — a beautiful young Polish girl with a seven-months-old baby whose GI father had been transferred home before his permission to marry had come down from his higher headquarters. After her departure, we resumed the gray watch on shut doors and moving curtains. (In all, some two thousand such "compassionate cases" were admitted from all of Europe.)

We knew what was happening in Poland long before newspapers published the State Department's protest against Communist coercion in the national elections of January '47 and the threat to break off relations with Poland's new government. Even before Christmas we were reading the portents in the faces of some of our repatriated Poles who reappeared again in the camp, usually tough single men like Tak Tak Schön who had had no families to impede their long nocturnal treks westward to the American Zone. It was like seeing ghosts. Faces we had waved good-by to in the fanfare of repatriation transports months before were glimpsed occasionally in our holiday crowds, and when we stared with quickened attention, fleshing out some gaunt countenance to the rounded contours our memories conserved, the face would turn away and extinguish itself in the anonymity of the back of a head. The returnees were illegally in the Zone, in the camps. They stayed only long enough to whisper their warnings to trusted friends and then disappeared into the vast moil of uncatalogued refugees called "free-livers," who lived outside the camps and were not then the concern of our organization. (Later on, when all but the special camps would be closed and when all DP's would be living on the German economy, Tak Tak and other self-reliants like him would come again into our fold as wards of the United Nations, eligible for emigration to countries other than the U.S.A., but we did not know that as we glimpsed their ghostly faces.) Their whispered warnings came eventually to our ears. We heard stories about Mikolajczyk's sturdy Polish Peasant Party with its back to the wall and of a tremendous Communist-controlled police ready to padlock every party except its own in the coming elections. Right after the New Year, more than a fortnight before results of the elections in Poland would be known, our DP's suddenly boycotted a "nationality screening" that was going on all over the Zone by order of Army and UNRRA, under the auspices (in the case of the Poles) of a group of Polish liaison officers attached to American Third Army and accredited to Warsaw. Our Poles simply sat down and refused to present themselves to the Polish officers for a one-minute interview and the showing of some such paper as a birth or baptismal certificate proving Polish nationality. In vain we called mass meetings, explaining that this screening was our only way of knowing how many Poles (and Balts, Ukrainians, Yugoslavs, and so on) our organization was caring for in the Zone. In vain we explained that there was no forced repatriation back of this simple nationality verification, that after a man proved by the showing of a single paper that he was a Pole, he would not have to repatriate to Poland unless he wished. Right then, if we had known how to read the signs, we would have seen our DP's ceasing to be people; they were fast becoming a political issue.

Pierre and the other Europeans on our team, who were more accustomed to living their history than to reading about it afterwards, understood why Warsaw had become a synonym for Moscow in the minds of the Poles. With a stubbornness which I could not define, I resisted the idea that Poland was ending as a free democracy. I kept seeing the miles of boxcars of Poles safely repatriated out of the half-world of the DP camps, more than six hundred crammed cars from our camp alone since the previous spring, and even if, toward the end, we had had to bait those repatriants with mountains of free food to get them to make up their minds, even if I still squirmed inwardly remembering the tormented tempted processionals past the visual displays of the sixty-day food ration, I still thought that repatriation was better than stagnation. I had lived long enough with the DP's to know what would happen if we had to keep them rotting in the DP camps for another year. I clung to my belief that Poland would vote free, and refused to read the writing on the wall. I needed just one more lesson to teach me that you did not have to wait for newspaper reports to tell you when your world was falling apart. You had only to look at the people.

I looked at the seventy block leaders I had summoned to a meeting on orders from Pierre telephoned from our district regional H.Q. I had convened them to tell that the nationality screening was ordered continued and that the Polish liaison officers would report again to Wildflecken in three days. I was looking at a volcano but I didn't see it. The seventy pairs of Slavic eyes were leveled upon me with fierce concentration, cold as the blue ice shimmering outside the steamy windowpanes, eyes that knew why the meeting had been called and waited in frigid politeness only to watch being spoken the words that had been tapped off the central switchboard the night before. The Countess stood beside me ready to translate. I heard the copies of the official order rattling nervously in her hands. I searched for a smile on the faces before me. The faces of men I had sat with in crowded little rooms and blanket-hung cubicles, whose wives and children I had sneaked special-issue garments to, whose home-brew I had often sampled without impolite queries as to the source of it, stared back at me as impersonally as the crowned white eagle painted wall to wall, across the back of the room.

Slowly I began to read the prepared speech Pierre had dictated. The room was hazy with cigarette smoke by the time I came to the sanctions part. I had the impression that a smoldering barricade separated me from the men in the room when I read that severe sanctions, possibly even eviction from camp, would be taken against any person, group or organization that attempted to block the nationality screening. But at the end of my speech the leaders quietly filed past the rostrum and dutifully took the written orders to be posted in their blockhouses with the scheduled time when each house was to report for the screening.

"At least they didn't boo me off the platform," I said to the Countess.

"It might have been better if they had. I don't like their quiet. And the camp, have you noticed?" She shivered in her blanket coat as we crossed the icy deserted street.

"Oh, people stay indoors in weather like this," I said. "This is the worst winter in fifty years of German memory. Papers say this cold wave came down from Siberia."

It was indeed as if a new Ice Age had descended over Europe. We had had three weeks of below-zero weather without a break. Three days from now, I thought, when we will have pulled the people out of their warm houses for the screening, we can expect our hospitals to begin filling up with grippe and pneumonia cases.

I looked at the people again three days later, but not at the people I expected to see. From the window of the mess hall of Kitchen 7, where the nationality screening was to take place, I looked down on a few shawled housewives outside the kitchen entrance with pails to receive their morning coffee brew. The inhabitants of Block A-4 were not queued up as scheduled.

Londa, representing Welfare, and Jock, our recently attached Eligibility officer, stood with me at the window peering out like anxious hosts. Behind us the party was building up. The four Polish liaison officers were opening their briefcases at the long tables and laying out stamp pads and seals that said "Polish Liaison Officer for Repatriation." Their military magnificence made us, in our quasi-military outfits with bits and parts from all the Allied nations and no brass buttons allowed, look like the stepchildren of the Occupation. Masses of gold braid curlicued over the visors of their officers' hats and their handsome long greatcoats swung amply over calf-high Polish boots.

"D'ye suppose the blighters have fouled us up again?" Jock whispered, looking at his wrist watch.

"Block A-4 is our gentry, teachers and actor people," said Londa. "We counted on them not to act like scared sheep."

"Maybe I'd better run down to the Polish committee and see what gives," I said. Ignatz was below with my car, looking over the splendor of the black Mercedes sedan with the Polish mission insignia emblazoned on its gleaming door panels.

The camp streets were nearly empty as we drove toward the committee building. Routinely, while waiting for the chief quartermaster to appear, I telephoned to Pierre in headquarters. Pierre cried danger into the phone. "Don't stay up in camp. Bring Londa and Jock down. There's a big demonstration forming. I've called in the constabulary."

"The constabulary?" I thought he had lost his mind. We had never yet called in the military to help us out in a pinch. I started to argue with him and he hung up. Ignatz drove me back to Kitchen 7. There were people now in all the streets, mostly men in small compact groups issuing from the blockhouses and walking in measured order toward the kitchen. I had been gone from there hardly a quarter of an hour but in that time nearly a thousand people had massed around the mess hall doorway as if sprung from the trampled snow. There were streamer banners on tall poles saying *Away with the agents of Moscow,* and I saw red and white arm bands but had no time to identify the ringleaders. I told Ignatz to park far back and I walked into the solid crowd. It opened like a Red Sea before me and I heard huzzahs for "Aunty UNRRA" as I mounted the steps.

Inside the mess hall the Polish liaison officers were surrounded by shoving Poles and Londa was yelling "You bloody idiots, get out of here," pushing at the DP's who pushed at the officers. I had just time to shout to the Polish captain, "The director is coming with constabulary," before he and his men were jammed into a single unit and jostled toward the door by a phalanx of demonstrators. Jock was at the mess hall windows hammering down on the fingers of Poles trying to climb in and I ran to another opened window and slammed it shut, but the incoming Pole pulled his wool cap down over his head and butted it through. The sound of shattered glass joined to the roar of the crowd outside. Then men poured in through all the windows while I brushed broken glass off my bosom. I looked out the jagged hole above the spot where the Polish mission car was parked. Buffeted and mauled, the Polish officers had gained their car. They got into it while its windows were being smashed. One of the officers got out to dislodge the ruffians who were rocking the car and I saw hands snatch off his gold-braided hat and start tearing at the insignia on his greatcoat; then suddenly he disappeared before my eyes. I thought for one horrified moment that the Poles had him underfoot stamping on his face. Pierre appeared with four jeeploads of armed constabulary, but from where he was at the far edge of the howling mass, he could not see the mission car or what was happening to it. It was being rocked violently by a five-deep cordon of strong-arms until it pitched into motion pointing downhill away from the street where the constabulary jeeps were stalled by a living wall. I saw the mauled Warsaw officer climbing or being dragged into the rocking car just as the mob closed in to give it the final shove that sent it careening down the icy hill toward the main gate.

A week later the *Stars and Stripes* brought us the headlines on the rigged Polish elections, a dull anticlimax hardly worth the reading. The relationship between that election event and what our visiting topside chiefs and Army brass called a hooligan demonstration against the nationality screening seemed difficult to explain or make understood. If we began our account by saying, "It really all started last spring when the Polish eagle lost its crown..." we were looked at as if we were candidates for the psychiatrist, not yet in the dangerous hearing-voices stage but certainly well advanced in the seeing-things stage.

That was how you learned to read the writing on the wall back there in 1947 in the middle of Occupied Germany. Only the first time it was difficult to believe what your eyes took in. After that, you got used to having History give you its previews in the living lexicography of fleeing people. Before the year would end, we were going to be reading, as matter-of-factly as a mariner reads storm clouds, the fall of Czechoslovakia months before it actually happened, reading new streams of stylish refugees from Prague and Pilsen descending upon us as if for a hastily decided week-end visit, gloved, hatted and modishly clad but with only a single leather bag in their hands. We would open special camps to house them, and eventually add a new column to our Nationality Breakdown reports and caption it *Czechs*. By the time the first frightened Jews from Berlin would start coming across, advance gray headlines heralding the coming blockade and the thundering Berlin airlift that was to follow (and bring out other refugees on the empty return trips to Rhine-Main), we would be so accustomed to the face of doom that it would seem like family to us.

Early in that bitter despair year of 1947, the DP camps were closed to newcomers. We understood the logic of this order. We knew even more vividly than our remote policymakers that somewhere an end had to be declared, a dateline bracket placed around the growing refugee mass; but it was heartbreaking for the field workers to have to say no to the late-comers who knocked at camp doors begging food, housing and United Nations care. Londa and her Welfare had the task of interviewing the new arrivals and telling them that the camp was closed, that all they could do was go down to Würzburg, register themselves in our newly established "Control Center" and then go out as a free-liver on the poverty-stricken German economy and wait until some door to a Western democracy would open and give them perhaps a chance to compete in the emigration requirements. Chouka and I went to Londa's room one night when we heard her weeping in frustration after her day in the welfare office.

"You tell them to be sure and keep Control Center informed of change of address. Change of address on the German economy!" Londa's drawn face had no fight left in it. "When you move from this cave to that rubble pile, be sure to give us your change of address. Someday maybe there'll be an emigration scheme. Maybe you'll qualify, if you don't have TB by then."

"There's Belgium," I reminded her. "Maybe it's not much, but it's a beginning."

Belgium had offered to take twenty thousand coal miners. The deal had been signed as long ago as January and soon, now, the Belgian mission would start recruiting in the Zone. It was the first door to open to our displaced, the only hopeful sign in that desolate spring.

"Belgium won't be for those people I sent away today." Londa jabbed at the smoking brown coal in her little iron stove. "They'll rot in their rubble piles till all the in-camp peoples are emigrated. Bead the directive, preference to camp livers. Anyway, what's twenty thousand against the eight hundred and fifty thousand we've still got sitting around in the camps?"

I imagined that all over the Zone the welfare workers were grieving like Londa, counting the four hundred camps still existing in Germany and then waiting in misery for their own small quota to be announced. Freedom was rationed too. There just wasn't enough of it to go around.

"The bloody little quota we'll get, a drop in the bucket."

"Allez, Londa." Chouka came in with three glasses of *genièvre,* the last of her Belgian gin. "Drink to Belgium. *Quand-même..."*

"Rotten of me to talk that way. But you get so crazy waiting for something big to happen." Londa lifted her glass. "Bless your battered little country, Chouka." Presently she gave a wry smile.

"You know what? We're going to have difficulty filling that coal-mining offer," she said.

"My hospital administrator signed up, the one in Pediatrics," said Chouka.

"Because he's a single man. But ask the family men."

I remembered the way Ignatz's face had closed up when I explained to him that the families could not go forward with the men, that wives and children would have to wait for three months in the camps until the men had proved themselves in the mines; then Belgium would allow the immediate families to come in.

"Ignatz refused," I said. "He won't take the chance on leaving his family in the care of an organization that's folding up with nobody knowing exactly what's to follow."

Already there had been a twenty-five per cent cut in our teams, in preparation for the end of UNRRA in the summer. Some kind of new international organization was shaping up over our heads while we fled through our days of quadrupled work. All that we knew was that we had not yet received a white envelope with a handsome testimonial inside it thanking us for our labors in a great humanitarian cause and telling us we could now go home.

"A hell of a time for that first door to open," said Londa. "You wonder what kind of psychology operates on topside."

"Maybe none at all," I said. "Maybe they're just as desperate up there as we are in the field. Maybe they just take what they can get. Hobson's choice."

It was good to see Londa forgetting her DP's for a while as she told Chouka about a man named Thomas Hobson who lived in seventeenth-century England and rented out horses for a living. "The only condition he imposed on his customers," she said laughing, "was that they had to take the horse standing nearest to the door. That's Hobson's choice."

"'Obson's choice!" Chouka tried out the new phrase. "It describes those gray mining towns... Liège, Charleroi. All the same color, houses, faces, sheets on clotheslines, all color of coal dust. *Certainement,* it is not a promised land."

"Don't sound so apologetic," Londa said. "At least it will get a few of our people off this crippling dole of international relief. Then maybe *my* country will wake up and do something. Or Australia, or Canada. When I think of the empty spaces!"

"Think of me thinking about the three million square miles of my country," I said. "Places out West where you can drive a whole day and not see a human being, only jack rabbits and roving steer."

Sometimes in those long vigils of watching, like our DP's, those overseas doors, the lands we came from seemed to spread out indefinitely and the vast vacant spaces within their borders became completely inexplicable. Any single camp was a complete self-sustaining unit that could have been set down like a colony in any uninhabited spot with all its wheels ready to start turning instantly and no help from the outside needed. It seemed such a simple solution that you wondered, often with a nameless fright, why nobody except yourself had thought about it.

The DP's planted vegetable gardens as soon as the ice went out of Wildflecken's high ground. Wherever there was a plot of earth with no building upon it or road across it, vegetable projects sprouted up. Stanislawa set her PW women to work on a vast truck-garden to supply the hospitals with fresh greens. The whole camp became so passionately garden-minded that we had to write a new penalty into our local law and order code — one package of cigarettes deducted from the ration of any DP caught stealing another's tomato vines and transplanting them to his own plot. The gardening urge was a healthy new development, but the sprouting leeks, cabbages, beets and tomatoes unnerved me in a peculiar way. It was as if I were looking at a writing rooted in earth this time. The rows of seedling green spelled out what our DP's were thinking. "Most of us won't be going anywhere this year either, so we might as well grow the makings for a good bortsch meanwhile."

~ 12 ~

The gardens that Wildflecken found time to plant only in its second spring were already two years old in another type of camp in Germany which some of us were soon to see. In camps of people like the Balts and Ukrainians, whose homelands had been absorbed into the USSR even before war's end and who had never experienced the upheaval of mass repatriation, the gardens had perennials like gooseberry and raspberry bushes, and two harvests of leaves had already been plucked from their flourishing tobacco plants and cured on strings stretched in the sun across the face of the caserns in which the inhabitants had lived more or less continuously since the 1945 liberation. Here there were landscaping effects and the crests of lost lands like Latvia, Lithuania and Estonia grew out of the earth in floral designs with marigolds, pansies and begonias spelling out the national colors. These were the "hard-core" camps, where life had had a continuity such as we had never imagined in the tidelike turbulence of a repatriating Polish camp.

In these hard-core camps the workers were as perennial as the gardens. There was a camp organization which ran like well-oiled machinery with the same workers continuously in the same jobs, and theaters, choirs, schools and churches developed to a degree that made these camps seem like self-governing townships, each with an elected camp leader who functioned like the mayor of any small town. Sometimes, when I had traveled to meetings in these places, I had felt like a sourdough coming into civilization after a long spell in the wilderness as I had watched the UNRRA people press buttons and get things done without threat or cajolery or the persuasion of an extra pack of cigarettes to meet a directive's deadline. The hard-core camps were the show places to which visitors were taken. After purchasing in the colorful handicraft shops some gleaming box of Latvian marquetry or Cossack blouse of Ukrainian embroidery with months of continuous labor carved or stitched into them, the visitors would be photographed against the background of a splendid garden being pruned to bloom... through a second summer of waiting and watching.

I always returned to the lunatic land of our all-Polish camp with its here-today-and-gone-tomorrow turmoil, thankful that my lot had been cast in a place where at least something moved, exploded or happened every day, even if it was something that made my hair stand on end. It seemed less sad.

But UNRRA was dying, or "phasing out" as it was called. All during the spring of 1947, the map of DP Germany was being changed. Bigger areas with more camps under a single supervision were created. We heard that the phantom successor organization had only a fraction of UNRRA's budget, that only fifteen nations instead of UNRRA's thirty-nine were willing to go on feeding and caring for the DP's. We knew that the life we had lived together as a team, firm as a closed fist in times of crisis, was soon to end when Medical was ordered to give us a physical examination. "To look at teeth and fetlocks," said Londa, "to see which of us old war horses is good for the final lap."

Pierre was the first to know his future. He was going to a bigger job, in the French Zone, and would be stationed in Baden-Baden, where I could see him putting the last deft finishing touches to the transformation of that stolid German spa town into a rococo replica of Paris. There, he told us, he would have everything, including his new wife, who was not permitted to join him as a dependent in the American Zone, where only wives of Americans were welcomed. Besides his wife, there would be the matchless trout and wines of the Black Forest, gala concerts in the Kursaal and plenty of risky roulette in the casino, which his own French Army of Occupation had already turned into an elegant officers' club (with no *sales boches* allowed), where every night you could dress in high tra-la-la and lose your silk shirt or win a million. There, under an Occupation that knew how to treat an ex-enemy, he could bellow at the Germans as they had bellowed at him when they had occupied Paris... *fini* this American Zone hocus-pocus about brotherly love and all is forgiven!

"There," he said, raising his goblet of golden Eschenberger to his assembled team, "I shall have everything — *tout ce qu'il y a de plus beau! Tout... tout...*" He drank his wine and began to cry. "Everything... everything," he mourned hoarsely, "except you, *mes enfants...* and this crazy *foutu* wild place that I shall never forget... never till the last great never."

The rest of us waited nervously. We were still too remote from our headquarters to know precisely what was going on. We worried about it like the DP's. The news from above struck us like pieces of wreckage drifting down past the popping eyes of deep-sea fish, incomprehensible shapes of things from an unimaginable surface world. We felt the stresses of shrinkage and streamlining and eventually they reached the field. When Pierre departed in glory for Baden-Baden, a new director came to appraise us, to switch us around in a consolidated area that now included almost half of Bavaria. The new director was an American named Sam and, he warned, he expected to be called Sam and not Uncle Sam — which told me that he too had suffered about his do-nothing country. We knew he was a field man like us who had been with the displaced persons operation since the beginning by the way he rapidly summarized where we stood and what we had to do with a greatly reduced personnel "from here on out." That was the only phrase we dared to use when we talked about time and the DP's. He gave us a tough brief talk in front of a map, pointing first to the town where he would establish his Area H.Q., then to the towns to which some of us would be transferred.

"This is where you're going," he said to me. His finger stopped at Aschaffenburg on the River Main. I remembered the town where an Area meeting had recently been held. I saw the wide highway dropping down into it from the low Spessart Mountains, the five Wehrmacht caserns, gray and pocked from machine-gun fire, on the outskirts where the hard-core DP's lived, and the shelled city at the foot of the highway where the bend in the river gleamed behind bombed red walls of an early seventeenth-century castle with its four square stone watchtowers still intact.

"I'm putting you in charge," said Sam. "Good setup. Ukrainians and Estonians mainly. Any questions?"

"When...?" My throat closed on the rest of it. I could no more imagine leaving Wildflecken than I could imagine my own death.

"In a couple of days, soon as you can turn over the files to the man I'm sending in here. The Belgian mission is coming first to Aschaffenburg. You'll have to pick it up fast to be ready."

"And the team... over there?"

"Four, all good. But you'll need another nurse and welfare. Got any preferences?"

Four officers in a spot that I knew had had fifteen to run it before. I reached for the best and named Londa and Chouka. Sam nodded and scribbled a note.

"Only don't start yelling for them right away," he warned. "Need time to find replacements for here."

I began to feel that I could work for a man like that, who did not have an if, but, or maybe in his vocabulary. I began to think what it would be to have camps of my own to run. I planned to sneak out of Wildflecken like a black border-crosser in the night. I knew I could never face up to an official farewell with my Poles.

Two days later I walked into the headquarters office in Aschaffenburg and laid my file of directives on a handsome walnut desk. I was on my own to sink or swim. It brought no comfort to think of the scores of other UNRRA "war horses" all over the reorganized areas who were doing the same thing I was at that moment, swallowing their fright and staring at a wall map that described the greatly enlarged corner of the DP world they were to take over. The experience that had accreted like an inner skeleton, rigid and strong as a coral ring, was all that held me up as I learned that I had nine thousand DP's of five nationalities scattered through seven camps, two of which were down the river miles away from the town. Then I sat down behind the desk and pressed a button. A tall blond lad, lean and handsome, entered and bowed.

"Are you the interpreter?"

"Not the chief one," he said in perfect English. "Only for the Estonians, madame. A minority group here. The director's interpreter was Ukrainian, the majority."

"And where is that one?"

"Your predecessor took her with him."

"Fine, then I'm taking you for chief. What's your name?"

"Helmut, madame." He flushed with emotion and bowed again. Then in the formal speech of a Baltic baron he said, "I am honored far beyond my merits, madame."

"I'll decide that later," I said. "Sit down now and fill me in. Fast. We've got a big day ahead."

A week later that first day ended and I was afraid to look in a mirror. I was sure I had talked myself blue in the face trying to win friends and influence people, for such was the business of "take over."

I had talked with the seven camp leaders, who ran their camps like little Tammany townships and looked like a group of business executives reporting in for a board of directors' meeting; with the five national group representatives, who fought for preferences for their individual nationals and thought my way of viewing them all simply as displaced persons quite old-fashioned; with bearded Orthodox priests, splendid in gold chains and jeweled crucifixes and tall turbans veiled at the back; and with the more practically garbed Roman Catholic priests in black soutanes and the Lutheran ministers in neat frayed business suits. I talked with the local Military Government officers and with the CIC, who roamed the camps on their mysterious business of counterintelligence, and picked up tales of intrigue that would have scared me to death had I believed the half of it. I talked with Georgi, the chief of my two hundred and fifty DP police, a handsome sharp-eyed Ukrainian with sweeping handle-bar moustaches, and I learned on inspection trips with him not to jump when his gate guards snapped to taut salute and clacked their boot heels together with the sound of pistol shots. During that week's talkfest, I learned many more things than the names, faces and dispositions of the people who would either work with me or against me. I learned that the Estonians had their remarkably low birth rate because they did not believe that this was a world into which you should bring children if you could help it, that the White Russians preferred to be called Nansenists or Stateless, and that they hired Germans (with cigarette wages) to fill their quota for woodcutters for their camp because 85 per cent of them had university degrees and had never held a work tool in their hands, and that the Ukrainians, proud, arrogant and extremely intelligent, could cry just as easily as the Poles had wept for their uncrowned eagle, when they talked about their Ukraine and its golden oceans of wheat under a wide blue sky, like their two-barred flag of blue and yellow which always had to fly blue stripe uppermost, the sky above the wheat. I learned, in sum, that the wider frame of many camps and many nationalities did not change the DP picture but only enclosed more variations on the single familiar theme of Displaced.

"It's just a continuity of everything you know already," I said to Londa and Chouka when they arrived looking anxious. "A continuity with push buttons and landscaping, that's all."

They brought me my personal continuity in the form of Ignatz, who had wangled a transfer to the Aschaffenburg motor pool when he heard I was using a Ukrainian driver. I stamped his authorization for room space in our one small Polish camp, happy that my human calendar had followed me, to remind me with wild flowers and mushrooms of the changing seasons and with new offspring of the accumulating years. He would have three children when his family would arrive the next month, he informed me with a bow. It was possible, I thought worriedly, that by the time the United States would open its doors, if it ever did, his family might then be so large as to be considered an economic risk under the support of a single wage earner.

The first break in the melancholy continuity of waiting for emigration doors to open was not the arrival of the Belgian mission as we had anticipated. There was to be a little curtain raiser first, a peculiar parody of the real purposes of emigration which the press overseas would jubilantly report as the affair of "The Flying Virgins." It began in Aschaffenburg on an afternoon in April when Helmut ushered into my office a dapper little man with a lisp and a limp and a great big briefcase in his hands. He was followed by Father Tomascewski, the priest from our Polish camp, and by a uniformed member of one of the big voluntary agencies headquartered in Frankfurt. I was introduced to the man with the limp, His Honor, a member of parliament from the Province of Quebec, who had come all the way over to Germany on a mission of mercy to recruit one hundred single girls of spotless moral character for his spinning mill in a small town in Quebec. Since the girls must be of Roman Catholic faith, he had first stopped by our Polish camp and discussed his purpose with the Father.

"But has there been clearance for this project from Zone?" I exclaimed.

"By telephone," said the voluntary agency man. "It's O.K." He nodded at the M.P., who was opening his briefcase to show his credentials. I looked at a letter from the prime minister's office in Ottawa, introducing His Honor, who was also a well-known industrialist who required textile workers for his mills. The Canadian Government stated that immigration requirements would be lifted to permit immediate entry of the young girls, since it considered this a worthy cause.

"Sorry, but *I've* not had clearance from our Zone H.Q. I can't let you go into that camp until I get the green light." I pulled from my file and exhibited the directive forbidding unauthorized visits of emigration officials to the DP camps, a protective measure written no doubt with an eye on some rugged industrialist overseas who would one day look at the DP camps and see them for what they really were — immense pools of manpower representing every known skill.

Father Tomascewski, who had been gazing at the M.P. as if he were the Angel Gabriel, gave me a look of shock. Rapidly and imploringly in German he explained that His Honor had come all the way from Canada to select the maidens, that he had chartered a plane to fly them from Frankfurt to Quebec and that he had only this one afternoon to interview. How could I, who knew better than most what this camp life did to our young girls, refuse them this God-sent opportunity?

"But what about their families?" I asked the M.P.

"Unfortunately, we cannot consider families," he said. "Housing shortage, you understand. The girls will live in a dormitory safe in the hands of a sisterhood."

I was sure then that there had been no authorization. UNRRA would never agree to separation of families after the years of struggle to reunite them. I reached for the phone to call Sam. While I gave the Area H.Q. number, I asked His Honor about wages and working conditions.

"The girls will receive the legal minimum," he lisped.

"How much is that?"

"Twenty cents the hour," he said. "They can earn as high as nine dollars and sixty cents a week and will pay only six dollars to the sisters for their board and room weekly."

Father Tomascewski was nodding excitedly at the munificence of the wage. He was multiplying Polish zlotys by Canadian dollars. I stared at the wolf in philanthropist's clothing.

"I'll put this call through from switchboard myself," I said, hurrying from my office before the phone could ring there. I needed elbow room and shouting space for what I had to say.

"So *that's* where that character is," said Sam when I had stopped to catch my breath. "A reporter from *Time* lost his trail in the Zone. Says he wants virgins..." Male laughter roared into the phone.

"Virgins?" Then I raved. We field people were not going to have any part in a deal like that and if our H.Q. was going to allow industrial wolves like Hizzonner to come into the camps and scoop their rivals on cheap labor then it was time we put on our hats and got the hell out of it since we were hardly qualified to be brokers for coolie labor...

"Don't sound off so fast," Sam said. "It's *not* authorized as far as I know."

"Who then?"

"God, I don't know. But I'll find out, believe me." Sam's combat voice meant business. He was not going to let our DP's be sold down the river a second time if he could help it.

"Yes, but what do I do, Sam?" I thought of the M.P. sitting in my office with his embossed credentials and of our DP Father looking as if the pearly gates had swung open to some of his flock.

"Listen, why not let the guy go into camp and just talk to the girls, since he's got this far? You never know what might be back of a thing like this, crazy as it looks."

"From slave labor to slave labor!" I banged on the switchboard. "You don't have to be a crystal-gazer to know what's going to happen to those girls with three dollars a week spending money, most of which they'll probably send back here to their families."

"They won't be virgins long," sang out my director.

"Call back quick," I begged.

"*Schnell* as hell," Sam said. "And listen, if that *Time* fellow phones in here again, I'm going to put him directly on to you."

"Me? Do you mean it? You mean I can talk?" It had been a basic rule since the beginning that we in the field must not talk to the press. We had even signed an agreement not to write articles for home consumption or to express any opinions publicly, as if we could not be trusted to tell the story of the DP properly. We only lived with him cheek by jowl.

"You tell 'em," Sam said. "Like you told me. Might do some good, you never can tell."

I walked back to my office spilling out so much anger in an imaginary conversation with the press that I was a model of diplomacy when I faced the M.P. I told him that he could go into the camp and talk with the girls, pending clarification from our Zone H.Q. Father Tomascewski wrung my hand.

"You'll come along, of course?" said the voluntary agency man. History is going to be written this day, said his shining eyes, even if your old granny organization takes its time to catch up with us.

"No," I said. "Got to wait here for an incoming call." I wondered when I smiled if I looked like what I felt like — a watchdog after its muzzle has been removed.

I never remembered what I said to the *Time* correspondent when he finally got through from Nürnberg. When you have been muzzled for more than a year, the first sounds emerging from a freed jaw don't seem to come from you but from some pent-up body of emotion living apart with no brain to roof it, no ribs to contain it. The clever factual article I read a month later in the May 19 issue of *Time* seemed to have no relation to my frenzied unburdening until I read it a second time and saw how the arrangement of the material built up the indictment "... pay them the legal minimum of 20¢ an hour... plans to spend $42,500 to fly the girls to Canada... In the House of Commons... labeled 'a fire sale of human misery'..." The "virgin" theme was mentioned with delicacy as if some man other than the one who had shouted gleefully over the telephone had written the story, "How's he going to find out? *Pinch* 'em?"

Not until the one hundred "hand-picked" girls arrived in Canada were they dubbed "The Flying Virgins" by a press that was parched, no doubt, for a human interest angle on that perennial bone-dry subject of the Displaced. The "experimental shipment" ended with the first hundred. The story died out of the news. But it took longer for hope to die in the hearts of the hundreds of Polish girls who had not been chosen, who straggled back to our camps from the big emigration assembly center in Frankfurt and would not unpack their wicker suitcases for weeks, or resume their jobs in kitchens, nurseries and sewing shops, but held themselves like faithful foolish virgins in instant readiness for the second coming of His Honor, who had promised to take them also into his kingdom of sweated labor, just as soon as he could secure permission for a second shipment.

(Some two years later, a follow-up report on these girls appeared in *The Survey*. The girls were doing fine, it said, many of them having moved on to other jobs when they had honorably completed their spinning-mill contracts — a Q.E.D. to the proposition that nothing can hold back a Flying Virgin if she is Polish.)

The arrival of the Belgian mission in early May was like a clean breeze blowing through stagnation, preceded by a flurry of paper. We posted the paper on the bulletin boards — copies of the mine contract, conditions of work (same rights as all Belgian miners, same compensations in case of injury), average earnings (five to seven dollars daily and up to fifteen if a man worked Sundays overtime), agreement on wives and children being brought forward after the three-month proving period and age limit up to forty years. In our seven camps we saw in microcosm what was happening all through the DP world of Germany at that moment — the lifted faces as to a fresh breeze, the tense debating wherever men were gathered, the quiet wives standing aside waiting to see if decision for a risky separation was to be made (some praying for it, some planning to override it) and the stricken look of the men over forty years, sad spectators of the first opening of a door to a new life for which they were already too old to qualify.

The mission men were as refreshing as their advance publicity. They pulled up at sundown on the scheduled evening in front of our billets and even before the vivacious Belgian colonel had put one stylish hand-sewn shoe across our threshold, he seemed to be part of our family, embracing our Belgian team members, introducing gaily his lieutenant in charge of security and his doctor who represented the mine syndicate, crying at our maid Sofia not to drop his briefcase that contained a bottle of fine *genièvre* gin and almost causing her to drop it when he added something in what sounded like fluent Russian. Our anxiety about protocol, about receiving our first mission without the experienced help of H.Q., vanished in the breeze of the colonel's appreciative comments on all he saw, on us dressed up to the nines, on the flowering plum trees in the garden, the guest rooms reserved for his party and the laden dinner table waiting. He brought a tape recorder to the table and set it going under his chair while he chattered in Russian with Sofia and lured her into startled exclamations and blushing denials. He played back her own voice as she was serving dessert and made her spill the strawberries and run shrieking from the room as from the devil himself.

Then he was ready to take on the DP's in the mass meeting we had laid on for him in one of our Ukrainian camps. We all went along with him, as if we were following an elegant and endearing Pied Piper who only masqueraded as a VIP colonel in charge of a mission.

The meeting hall in an old reconstructed warehouse held about six hundred and it was packed tightly with a murmuring throng from all seven camps, all five nationalities. Georgi, splendid in cavalry breeches tucked into high Ukrainian boots, met us at the door with a clack of heels and fought a way for us through the crowd of standees to the lighted stage where interpreters waited. I was glad that the colonel was not going to address the crowd in Russian. I wanted to hear each word of this first offer of a home and a job to the homeless and jobless.

The rationed electric bulbs hanging spottily around the auditorium dropped just enough light over the audience to reveal shawls and felt caps and an occasional beard when it was white enough to reflect out of the shadowy mass, and it seemed to me as I stood up to introduce the colonel that at least half the audience was either female or overage, that the young men who had already made up their minds and signed on for the mining scheme had stayed away to leave as many places as possible for the older ones to come and listen and realize that none of this could ever be for them, and I faltered every time I said *We*.

We have waited for this moment for nearly two years... In the front row lit clearer by footlights I could not see a single man young enough to swing a pick in a coal mine except the three Estonian veterans of a Baltic legion who had hobbled in on their iron crutches with their amputated leg stumps neatly sewed in trouser pouches. *We have waited for this first helping hand to reach through to us...*

The colonel stepped forward to the footlights and began to talk. He started immediately on the subject of wives. He had one himself. He knew what it cost to get away from her for three months. Only the war had made it possible for him. You heard young male laughter from the dim thicket of faces out front, then the crowd hushed while the colonel described what the German V-bombs had done to housing in his small country, which was part of the reason for the delay in bringing forward families of miners. Temporary housing shortage, and the toughness of the work. Coal mining was no bed of roses. A man must prove himself. If he could take it for three months, the chances were that he could take it for the two-year life of the contract. After that, he could renew his contract or seek other employment through the Ministry of Labor, though there were not many surface jobs available in Belgium. In five years he could elect to become a citizen of Belgium.

His hands flew about as if he were wrapping up an invisible package. You could feel all eyes on that airy package that contained a new life, an unheard-of wage, a hole in the ground to work in and citizenship eventually, citizenship with a real identity card to prove that a man belonged to one of the recognized branches of society and no longer to this unknown place of the displaced. The interpreters followed sentence by sentence in Russian, Ukrainian, Polish and Estonian, keeping their eyes on the package around which the expressive hands seemed to be tying a neat bow.

I couldn't look any longer at the faces of the three Estonian amputees in the front row, lifted toward the stage like lanterns with wavering lights in them. It was my first taste of the bitterness of selective emigration, my first look at the other side of the new-life coin. I thought of the hundreds like that, without legs, hands or arms, minus one eye or with dark spots on the lungs, which a recent medical survey had shown to be present in the Zone, many of them maimed after they had been brought into Germany and used to replace German workers in the danger spots under bombardment, and I wondered with miserable foreboding if there was a country on earth that would consider our cripples. It had taken almost two years to get this first life line thrown out to our able-bodied only.

I watched the colonel play a tape recording of Poles who had worked in the Belgian mines since before the war. Screams of delight and astonishment came from the audience as Polish words rolled from the little machine, with *dobre's* scattered like sighs of satisfaction through the talk. We *had* to get them all out of Germany, even those legless ones who were laughing and slapping their stumps, although they probably did not understand a word of the miners' Polish dialogue but only the wonder of workingmen's voices coming to them off a tiny tape from the great outside world.

The mission moved fast the next day and we moved with it. Our Medical gave the chest X-ray and VD clearance, our Employment produced the work-testing cards, and Georgi secured from the local Military Police the certification that none of the one hundred and eighty men who had signed for the first recruitment had ever been in jail. This was to be a propaganda recruitment, the colonel said, to get a few men from each camp as fast as possible to Belgium so they could write back and tell their friends about it. Then the serious business of filling the quota for twenty thousand would begin.

The mine doctor listened to hearts and examined eyes, made sure that each man had all ten toes and fingers and then passed him with a pat to the colonel at the end of the line who filled in the blank spaces on the mining contract and handed a copy to the successful candidate. Londa and I watched each step of the process, learning the new routine of getting people out, astonished and relieved to find that emigration selection was not really very different from the technique of an employment agency. You simply matched men to the job requirements. It looked like the cream of the crop that lined up afterwards, all husky young men with eyes alight for adventure, clutching their contracts as if they had the world by the tail.

"Just look at them," Londa whispered. "Look at those faces. Pays back some of our dreary days, eh what?"

The accepted miners listened to the colonel's briefing on the departure. Day after tomorrow at dawn, he said; we need you as badly as you need to get away from these camps. But they were away already. Their excited faces were the kind you see peering out windows of trains approaching a frontier, lively with eagerness to see the first cart, cottage or costume that tells something about the way of life in the new country. Happiness was such a rare expression on DP faces that you had to look away from it, toward the windows and beyond to the gray angles of a blockhouse scalloped with clotheslines slung across its pitted façade, to remember where you were.

It took us a day to co-ordinate everything, to get trucks from Army to move our men to the British Zone railhead where they would entrain with others bound for Belgium, to make sure that each man had all the right papers (after the night of festive farewells our miners were as nervous as brides and talked in voices an octave higher than normal) and that he turned in his camp registration, food and clothing cards and signed a receipt for the blankets he would be allowed to take with him.

Departure day dawned for us at four-thirty, when alarm clocks went off in the billets. We had just enough officers to cover the five camps from which recruits were to be picked up by our own trucks and conveyed to our Polish camp where the Army trucks would be lined up. I headed a convoy of four trucks into one of the Ukrainian camps where forty-nine men were waiting. Their wives, sweethearts or parents were out with them in the half-dark, with flowers. There were so many hands to help hoist bedrolls, bicycles and suitcases aboard that we were ready to go within fifteen minutes and I led them right out because I could not endure more of the hand-wringing and final embraces either. It seemed when I glanced into my rear-view mirror that I was convoying four truckloads of statues down the highway, standing statues of men all faced backward toward the camp with stiff bunches of flowers upright in motionless fists.

The promised fifteen Army trucks were lined up smartly in a double row across the parade ground of the Polish camp, with a few Poles including Ignatz standing about as spectators, evoking in me a momentary nostalgia for Wildflecken, to which the whole Polish quota in this first recruitment had been given. Londa came in with her convoy, then the others followed in the split-second timing we had planned, with the priest truck and the band truck bringing up the rear.

Quickly and quietly in the gray light the transfer was made and the UNRRA trucks pulled away leaving only the double line of the big GMC's filled with men standing now so clear against a dawning pink sky that you could see which ones were mopping their eyes, which ones were leaning down over the side rails to clasp hands with the women who had run ahead to this final departure point, and here and there a young father holding a baby that had been passed up to him from the thronged shadowland between trucks.

The priest's truck backed and centered to face the GMC's. The Greek Orthodox and Greek Catholic priests removed their black turbans, put on magenta caps and raised their tall wood crosses. From where we stood on the ground the whole thing was lifted against the dawn sky — the dark crosses, the brilliant magenta caps and the rows of young men standing bareheaded and motionless in the trucks, listening with gravest intensity to what was doubtless the last service they would hear in their native tongue for a long time. They bowed low and crossed themselves at the final prayer and then watched in utter silence while their priests climbed from the altar truck to pass down the lines of GMC's and sprinkle holy water on each flat green hood. We followed the progress of the priests by the bared heads ducking in unison as the processional passed each truck. It was as if an invisible hand were brushing low over the vehicles one by one, bending the sky-limned heads with a brief light touch.

The last truck was blessed, the band struck up, the motors roared and there at last was our convoy moving out bumper to bumper under the flag-draped arch of the camp's gate. It was just fifteen Army trucks carrying only a handful of no-longer-displaced out that gate for the last time, but to me it looked like a great green dragon in the dawn with one hundred and eighty brave men riding astride it, beating it with their wildly waving arms until it smoked to speed and disappeared, a streak of green down the deserted highway.

We stood for a moment staring at the tire tracks curving out the gate as, when an emotion has swept through a crowd, people stare at any shape or mark that was in the scene at the same time, seeming to ask themselves if this or that was the cause of it, seeking to tie the rush of feeling down to something substantial, and only the whimpering of the ninety-day widows was heard in that momentary trance when we tried to catch up with what had just happened.

A page had been turned at last. Those marks in the dust were something more than tire tracks. They were a new script spelling out the beginning of the end and they would go on and on through the coming months, tracing out the continuing story of more departures for Belgium, of departures of lumbermen for Canada, of common laborers for Australia, textile workers for England and Holland, public health doctors for Venezuela, domestic workers for France, until at last there would seem to be no place on earth to which those tread marks did not point, except to the United States of America.

And between the lines of that purposeful print you could see the camps aging and growing sadder as the old people, the cripples and the ailing would be left behind, with the masses of children of the too-large families that were seldom selected and most often were not even qualified to apply, since so many of those emigration schemes would call for single persons with no dependents. In those gray spaces between the lines you could see country after country reaching in for its pound of good muscular workingman's flesh and you could even see yourself eventually being grateful for the world's hasty humanity that took the strong and left the weak because it meant at least that some got out each time. And, since hope was a habit with the DP's, they would not cry out at the injustice that selected muscles instead of mind, but would be glad each time another group of candidates made the grade and would flock to watch each thrilling departure with the thought written clear as a neon flash across their yearning faces, *Possibly this too can happen to me someday.*

The bright moving morning of our first emigration transport ended on a note unexpectedly forlorn and solitary. An elderly bachelor who had risen early with his roommates, as if to join the departure watchers, walked off into the nearby woods and hanged himself. It was estimated that he had been dead three hours when children saw the shape swinging dark against the lacy lightness of Maytime woods and ran crying to the DP police, who cut him down and brought him back to camp. The man had dressed neatly and completely for his final departure and had put all his essential papers together in one coat pocket, as if to spare us the trouble of guesswork and make it easy to report promptly to military authorities that Displaced Person No. 235,456, Ukrainian, male, born 1882 in Kiev, agronomist by profession and without kith or kin, had that morning committed suicide, no motive apparent.

I did not see the connection between that solitary act and our mass departure for Belgium until I was telephoning my transport report to Area headquarters and heard myself adding the suicide incident like a footnote to the new page that had been turned that day.

"Sam, it's almost as if..."

"Sure it is," said Sam. "It's what we've been predicting every time we go up to Zone H.Q. and there'll be plenty more of it from here on out unless someone has the guts to stand up to some of these muscle-gathering missions and make 'em see the light. Poor old guy," he said in a different tone. "Sixty-five and no son or daughter to help him get out as a dependent."

"On the Incident Report... what'll I write in for motive?"

"Despair," said Sam harshly and hung up.

So despair was the footnote and that too would go on and on, not appearing on every new page turned but scattered here and there and taking every strange form to express the thwarting, going even to the bitter extreme of denunciation of the people chosen by the people left behind — a word dropped or an anonymous letter hinting of collaboration, which could hold a candidate frozen in the security check for months and months or even exclude him finally... but that was still a long time off. It would not be until the United States scheme would open up that denunciation would become the malevolent indoor sport of the rejected ones. You could not imagine such human blight, in those early emigration days, when you wrote up your first footnote on frustration and believed that despair manifested itself only in one way, in a quiet gentlemanly act of self-extinction involving only a single soul.

~ 13 ~

During the summer of 1947, uncertainty hung as menacingly over our heads as it hung over our DP's — a protracted period in which we seemed to have no more future than they. On June 30 the twice-extended time of UNRRA finally ran out and our United Nations organization changed horses midstream — a nerve-racking maneuver when you had your arms full of children of the DP miners who had gone off to Belgium, with their worried wives fearing that you also might vanish as the familiar red trappings of UNRRA were vanishing from signboards and directional arrows all over the Zone. The blue life-preserver insigne of the successor IRO (International Refugee Organization) was painted over our headquarters, over camp gates and on the hoods of all our official vehicles. The scenery for the last act, the final phase, was set up swiftly as if something totally new were about to begin.

But the same actors moved across the boards of that immense DP stage. Two years after war's end there were still almost a million DP's living in the camps of Europe, of whom more than half were in our U.S. Zone. There were also many of the same old stagehands left around, pioneers of UNRRA's first relief teams, willing to go on with the show and use their sad know-how of caring for homeless masses. It still seemed like the most important show on earth, despite the fact that some of its road companies were offering real shocker performances, notably the one in Israel, where already half a million Jewish and Arab refugees were piling up in camps that made our scaly shot-up German barracks seem, in comparison, like palaces. News pictures startled us with their poignant familiarity, though outwardly the homeless hordes of burnoosed Arabs and Jews bore little resemblance to our European refugees. It was startling to realize that before our own original mass of displaced had been resolved and resettled, another was forming on another part of the planet as if Displaced were a disease like running sores that could break out anywhere and had become the accustomed ailment of the century.

From the frequency of troop transfers out of Germany to the Orient, you could even believe that something more than an Occupation might be building up over there, but fortunately at that point, your most discouraging imaginings could never foresee the news items which, just three summers later, would begin to appear in the IRO field bulletins... *Polish-born ex-DP Wasyl Mazwijko aged twenty-one killed fighting with American forces in Korea; Latvian-born ex-DP Janis Akmentins aged twenty returned from Korea to sponsor in Minnesota, a double amputee with Purple Heart...*

All around the charmed circle of our DP world portentous events were crackling like lightning, giving us the impression of living inside a great glass globe where nothing was happening except the long slow drag of waiting for something to happen. The literate Balts, Ukrainians and White Russians watched the doors of America in that never-ending summer of 1947 exactly the way I was watching them. Their national group leaders subscribed to American periodicals and the Paris edition of New York newspapers and they read articles about themselves with disquieting captions like "The Faceless People" and "DP's Are Not Dangerous," and showed the fund-raising advertisements of American charities which pictured the DP's in rags behind barbed wire with begging hands extended toward the reader.

"How will we ever get to America with a presentation like that?" they asked me. Even German newspapers, coming to life under the wary surveillance of Military Government, gave them a bad press. Occasionally the Germans slipped in some bitter complaint about the cost of feeding those "fascists in DP camps," and now when our people sought refuge on the grassy riverbanks of the Main to fish for eel, they hunched over their long willow poles and watched their lines with bleak fixed stares, pretending not to hear the German fishermen shouting at them from rowboats midstream: *"Why don't you go back to your Volga River where you belong?"*

Inside the hard-core camps, in the only places on the planet that were safely theirs until tomorrow, the DP's lived their startlingly real shadow life just as if it had connection with the outside world and were an intrinsic competitive part of it. Rival camp newspapers fought out camp elections with impassioned fury. New businesses sprang into existence to undercut established concessions like barber and cobbler shops, synthetic lemonade stands and beer gardens. Just as in the outside world, men occasionally seduced each other's wives and the camp lawyers' briefcases bulged with marital troubles. Knives flashed in brawls over room space and camp doctors sewed up the losers. Even the clothing-distribution warehouses were set up like countered stores, with a men's, a women's and a children's department and a curtained dressing room where the garments of international charity could be tried on before acceptance. Visitors always stared with astonishment. They had not expected to find camp life so "normal." They could not recognize the gestures of *As if...*

Until the Baptists came to Aschaffenburg, I had less hope in a migration to the States than the DP's themselves, but I had plenty of space to hide my despair from their probing eyes because I was totally empty inside. The Baptists came in the middle of the hot humid Main Valley summer, two top-ranking leaders of that faith which we had thought was perhaps the only one not represented in the DP world. We learned to our surprise that among our Ukrainians, whom we had lumped together in haste as being mainly Orthodox, there was a small group of Baptists. A fanfare of advance warning from Sam's headquarters indicated VIP treatment for our visitors from Stateside. Then the two homespun men of God came to our camps as naturally and unpretentiously as if they were making a call on some neighbors. I had forgotten that Americans like that existed.

The senior pastor was white-haired and full of quiet vigor. He spoke with an accent that reminded me of the tall-corn states, and when he stood on the platform of our crowded meeting hall and uttered the first real words of hope for an American emigration scheme which we had heard that year, he was instantly believable. The faces of our DP leaders seemed to pale as they listened, as if the shock of believing again were almost too much for them. The pastor told how Americans in small parishes all over the land were saying that it was a disgrace that the United States was moving so slowly — Protestant sects joining with the Roman Catholic, the Jewish and the Orthodox to say such things in all sorts of meetings and conferences, and there was a note of contained wrath in his friendly even voice like an echo from those distant parish halls where hundreds of angry letters to Congressmen were being composed.

"We are all working together to get a bill through Congress," he said, "and with the help of God we shall succeed."

The pastor looked at the strained faces of our diplomaed gentry — the editors, lawyers, doctors and leaders of all our nationalities and the priests of all our faiths; then he smiled as at an afterthought which had occurred to him.

"You know," he said gently, "you are not strangers to us. America was founded by the voluntarily displaced. We are a nation of the displaced from all the lands, from many more than you have represented here."

No one had ever before thought to tell them that. The simple words of fact hung momentarily in the air like a vision. It was as if the pastor had pushed open those watched shut doors of America just enough to give a glimpse of what lay behind them and, with startled recognition, the DP leaders peered through the crack at the powerful nation whose forefathers had been displaced people like themselves.

The total-immersion baptisms in the River Main took place a few days after the Baptist leaders had gone on to gather in their small flocks from among other camps in Germany. The baptisms were as unadorned as had been the great plain words of the voyaging pastor which had made America seem so breathtakingly inevitable. Our barefoot white-gowned refugees walking under willows toward the water as to the River Jordan were perhaps the strangest sight that had ever been seen in DP Germany, a ritual so devout that I was almost ashamed to photograph it but I knew that if I did not, I would never believe it afterwards.

Other holy men came to the camps that summer, bringing to our DP's as had the Baptists a different kind of food from anything the IRO could offer, and one for which they were immensely hungry. The visit of the Greek Catholic archbishop was preceded by a frenzy of preparation which involved the majority of our Ukrainian population. Evergreen trees from the Spessart forests were set up before the stone pillars of the camp's gate and garlands were looped from the overhead arch from which hung the papal banner of yellow and white. The River Main was fished clean of eels to be smoked for the banquet and fine white wines from the Würzburg vineyards were brought in by the barrel. Every camp street on which the archbishop would set his feet was strewn with rose petals, and when his black limousine appeared before the gate, the main street was a colored canyon solidly walled with reverent refugees in brilliant costumes with the kindergarten infants lined up in the front row looking more like flowers than children. I stood with my team in the receiving line feeling a bit strange in the midst of the alien splendor of the Eastern Church until I saw two American MP's loitering in their patrol jeep on the highway beyond our flowered gate, staring at our ceremony with a *What the hell goes on here!* expression, and I said back to their grinning windburned faces, *There's nothing queer about this, it's just one of the things that goes on over here without which our people would have perished long ago despite the shiploads of food... as if man could live by bread alone...*

His Eminence descended from the limousine. We had a glimpse of a portly man sashed in purple with a wise and worldly face. Then our DP priests closed in around him and helped to vest him in a magnificent scarlet satin cape striped in gold and a high cloth-of-gold hat embroidered with pearls. His deacon handed him his tall staff tipped by a gem-encrusted cross. When he turned around and walked toward us with the German sun shattering lights off all his gold and jewels, he was no longer a man, but an ikon come to life.

    The summer of 1947 was also a time of beginning "close-out." Closing a camp was a hideous business. It looked progressive in *Stars and Stripes* when you read that the Army had handed back another piece of confiscated property to the Germans and that the IRO was being most co-operative in its consolidation program, but behind the lines was heartbreak every time. Even when the camp to be liquidated was only a wood barrack shantytown like our White Russian center a few miles down-river from Aschaffenburg, a place from which you would have thought the DP's would run with joy, it was a little Eden in their eyes. Even if some of the inhabitants had been brought there originally to work in the wood-fiber artificial silk mill as slave laborers and had themselves helped erect the shabby shanties considered by the Nazis good enough to house OST people, the pain of those old associations had been overlaid by two years of security under United Nations care which had enabled them to beautify the one place on earth they were sure of, the one spot in which they had remained the most continuously since they had fled Red Russia after World War I and drifted around Europe with Nansen passports until World War II had caught and fixed them in this camp that had come to seem like home.

    I felt like a monster when I told our White Russians that their camp was closing and that within a week the boxcars would back into the siding to take them and all their belongings to a big Stateless camp in another part of Germany. I listened to the voice of Europe's uprooted talking to me from taproots sunk deep in that quiet private corner of the DP world and I wished that their spokesman had been someone other than the Russian noblewoman with white wings in the black hair swept back from a dreamy intellectual face. Her deep voice was more fitted to recite the poetry of Pushkin than the mundane tales of five thousand square meters of vegetable gardens just coming to maturity, of the toy and artificial flower shops which could be counted on to pay their way surely by Christmastime, of the sure employment in the fiber-silk mill where nineteen of their people, professors mostly, were already apprenticed and actually earning a few reichsmarks weekly at the spindles. For me it was a sort of death march to walk with that woman through the gardens and look at tomato vines so heavily hung with fat green globes that they had to be propped, at beets and leeks and herbs for bortsch and at untransplantable tobacco bushes knee-high and full of white blossoms. I followed her to the foot of the gardens where elderly DP men sat along the grassy banks of the River Main to fish for the carp that were just coming in following the eels, and I listened to how her small band of Old Russian *émigrés* could live without any help at all from us if only they could remain in the little Elysian economy they had created out of their former slave-laborer quarters.

So... the little cross-marks were put up on the new scoreboard recording camps liquidated and properties handed back to the Germans. Each successive close-out was as unbearable as the first, not only for the one who had to announce the evil tidings but for the entire team as well, since each department had to take back from its grieving counterpart its own inventoried properties — Supply its wardrobes, beds and blankets, Welfare its school furniture and material, Medical its camp clinic equipment and ambulance and sometimes a whole hospital that had to be dismantled and accounted for scalpel by scalpel — and if, toward fall, we began to look like frazzled housekeepers going crazy trying to make both ends meet, that was exactly what we were. More millions were about to be pared from the IRO budget for the U.S. Zone. We never knew why. We knew only that the small camps had to go because they were, logistically speaking, almost as costly to maintain as the big camps housing a thousand or more and that every possible cent that could be squeezed from the overall operation had to be channeled to the big resettlement centers soon to be established to house the many emigrant-recruiting missions that came to us thicker and faster as the summer days wore into autumn.

Every mail brought more austerity orders from the struggling new IRO as it endeavored to condense within its narrower financial frame the vast sprawling empire which UNRRA had created for the needs of the early days. Every new order that closed out a camp or cut a thousand DP workers from the payroll whittled flesh from the bones of the field workers. Londa's hacking cough was continuous now and Chouka was a walking case of jaundice, inspecting her camp clinics with yellow eyeballs but unable to take to bed until she had trained new batches of nurse-aides to replace the young DP girls who had recently emigrated to England as domestic workers. Our supply and transport men looked like ghosts of their former selves as their trained warehousemen and truck drivers emigrated to Canada as lumberjacks, to Belgium as miners, to Australia as common laborers.

The scramble of the DP's to get out of Germany was at once heartbreaking and humorous. The camp bulletin boards listing all the current avenues of escape made you think of some kind of macabre stock market that dealt in bodies instead of bonds. The DP's read the job offerings and rushed to qualify. When, for example, we posted the advance news that Canada would accept qualified tailors, everyone who had ever sewed on a pants' button was a master tailor. Our DP nurses with diplomas from Leningrad, Warsaw and Kiev swore they had done a bit of tailoring before they studied nursing. Ace mechanics in our garages dropped their tools and lined up at our employment office to try to have the record on their work-tested card changed from mechanic to tailor. Then the emigration directive came down to us with the exact requirements written in such technical garment-industry language that I could translate intelligibly only the single phrase — pocket-baster. And, instead of the quota of hundreds which we had hoped to get, we read that the total scheme called for just one hundred and sixty from the whole U.S. Zone, which, divided among all the areas and subareas, gave us in Aschaffenburg a quota of exactly six tailors to be selected from a population of nearly seven thousand of whom the majority were, at that moment, master tailors.

Again and again, we picked up and dusted off the rejected ones. Their reaction to rejection was immediate and total despair, as if a door had slammed in their faces and shut them forever in a dark room with no other egress. The more highly developed the DP, the more absolute was his hopelessness. One of our Ukrainian doctors, who performed some thirty major operations a week and seldom lost a case, wept like a child when he was rejected from a scheme calling for hard-rock miners for Canada. Helmut, my Estonian translator, came back rejected from the Australian mission for the same reason he had been rejected from the Belgian scheme — too many elderly dependents — and he lived in a state of stunned surrender for weeks, hugging his three old maiden aunts to his broad chest and asking me what kind of a world it was that expected him to plow under the last three relatives he had left on earth so as to establish his status as a single man with no dependents.

You felt like a crazy Quixote, telling such people to wait for the U.S. scheme when that long-debated emigration act was still but a spate of words in Congress and much more concrete events, which seemed to put a premium on time, were rumbling to completion just over the Zone borders. The DP's knew about the secret meeting in Poland that revived the Comintern in October '47, just as if they had attended in person and had heard every fiery speech denouncing "American imperialism" and the Marshall Plan. They measured the increasing streams of refugees from Czechoslovakia and gave that country just three months longer to live. Actually, they missed out on their prediction by about sixty days. Jan Masaryk did not "commit suicide" in Prague until March '48, but by that time, our DP's would no longer be worrying about so distant a danger. The Soviet land blockade of Berlin would be, by then, almost a *fait accompli,* with river barges already tying up for the duration along the banks of the Main and the Rhine where our DP's could go and look at them as at something happening in their own back yards.

We went on with our work just as if we had years of security ahead in which to accomplish our mission. Since the only fact emerging clear from the Congressional bickering was that every DP emigrant to the United States would first have to be assured of job and housing by some sponsor within the States, we began asking our DP's whom they knew inside the U.S.A. Even the most remote relative was a point in space toward which a letter could be directed. We passed out postage stamps and free advice on how to broach to a fifth cousin in Iowa (possibly with a mortgage over his head and ten dependents of his own to support) the subject of guaranteeing job and housing to some forgotten kinsfolk hopefully waiting reply in a DP camp in Germany. When a DP was too timid to write his own exploratory letter, we wrote it for him — Chouka for her nurses, Londa for her teachers and workshop people, our supply and transport officers for their drivers and warehousemen — so that finally we all became so emotionally involved in the mail-order campaign to find sponsors that we began to feel as displaced as the people whose causes we pled.

I looked with dread toward the prospect of a third Christmas with the DP's, to the lifting of small chipped glasses filled with pink schnapps and the toasts *May this be our last Christmas together in DP-land* which I knew would choke in the throat if I had to utter them for a third time. The news from Washington was not good. It began to look as if Congress would recess without taking any action on the DP bill, except to shelve it. If replies to some of our letters had not begun to come in, we would probably have fled the camps over the holidays and gone off to Paris on the packed furlough trains.

The replies drifted in with the late November snows. They made me so homesick I could hardly bear to read them when the recipients rushed to my office waving them at me and begging to be shown on my United States wall map where was the city of Texas, the state of Minneapolis. Was the weather there like Latvia's? Were there forests like in Estonia? How many days did it take to get there by train from Neuyorke? First came a few air-mail letters from the richer relatives who could afford the air stamp, then bigger batches arrived by ship with five penny stamps across the face or a single sky-blue one with the profile of a President, and they were written on every kind of paper from heavy business bond to the ruled tablet pages torn from a nickel blankbook and in every kind of handwriting from spindly uncertain block print to fine-flowing script with shaded flourishes on the tops of the *T's* and the tails of the *Y's*. The postmarks made a kind of song as you riffled through the mail sacks... Grand Rapids, Little Rock, Saginaw, Cedar Falls, Lost Nation, Lexington, Eureka, Danbury, Pawtucket, Tecumseh, Hattiesburg, Athens, Paris, New London... Santa Rosa, Santa Monica, Saint Louis...

The letters were the first slender threads that connected a person with a place and although an emigration machinery so complex and tremendous that we could not even dimly imagine it would have to be set up before any of those threads could become a life line, we reacted as if the recipients already had one foot on the gangplank of a ship.

The day before Christmas, Ignatz received a colored postcard from a place he called Tchee-Kah-Goo. It was from a remote relative he had never seen in his life though he remembered vaguely having heard his mother speak of someone in the family who had crossed the River Bug one day long ago and had kept going westward until he was half around the world. Ignatz's hands shook as he translated his message from Mars. *Tell me what I should do to help — Basyli Sikorski.* He touched the Chicago postmark with wonder and ran his finger over the three one-cent stamps affixed crookedly in one corner. It never occurred to him that his relative had forgotten to give a return address until I pointed it out to him. He had thought that Chicago, America was enough.

But it was enough for me... to start on. That night I wrote my first letter of inquiry to Chicago to try to trace a name almost as common in Polish as Smith is in English. I began with the Chamber of Commerce. I would work through every agency I could think of, through telephone companies, Polish societies, trade unions and Catholic clubs. I told Ignatz sternly that he must immediately join one of the IRO classes for adults and study English, there was no time to be lost.

"Once that DP bill gets passed," I said, "things here will move like lightning. *Blitzen! Schnell!*"

My happy prediction seemed to frighten him. His blue eyes widened with worry as he studied my face for an instant. Then he cleared his throat and told me that he could not possibly leave Germany until the spring. His wife was expecting.

"What *again?*" I cried. It seemed only yesterday that he had shown me the crumpled yawning face of a new son.

"*Ja bestimmt!*" he said, trying modestly to conceal his pride.

I could see that I would need my advertising experience to sell Ignatz and his expanding brood to a distant relative who, when and if we located him in a city of four million, might not turn out to be rich enough to guarantee housing for a family of six.

~ 14 ~

When President Truman welcomed the three-hundred-thousandth DP into the United States in January 1952 and the chairman of the United States Displaced Persons Commission published his windup report on the greatest planned emigration in our history, I learned to my astonishment that it had cost each United States taxpayer only $1.93 for the three years' operation of the DP program which began in June 1948 when the DP Act was finally passed. I could hardly believe this, yet there it was in a newspaper with credit line attached. Chairman John W. Gibson reporting to the nation on what he so aptly called "a venomous postscript to World War II."

During those years my heart had sometimes bled for my fellow taxpayers as I watched the U.S. scheme expand from a simple emigration selection and processing program, such as had been going on quite normally with the Canadian, the Belgian and the Australian missions, into a gigantic three-ring circus, with so many people, organizations and societies getting into the act and so many new acts and pyrotechnics added that at last no single person could say where the thing began or ended and you were sure it was a show for which the Americans would go on paying, for generations, like Civil War pensions. But only $1.93 per taxpayer for all this...?

The arising of the Resettlement Center in the spring of '48, three months before the passage of the DP Act, sent waves of excitement through our vast sprawling area. We envied the workers who were attached to this new creation, which was going to be the stage on which "the Last Million" were going to make their farewell appearance as DP's. We heard that seven such centers were being readied in our U.S. Zone, scattered strategically through Hesse, Württemberg-Baden and Bavaria, and we could hardly wait to see our own in a Panzer casern on the River Main from which two thousand DP's had been recently evacuated. Our engineers and supply men, busy with the painting, altering and procurement problems of the new setup, talked like hysterical interior decorators working against time. At last something new had been added.

But when we had our turn at sight-seeing in our new Resettlement Center, we felt at first like busmen on a holiday. The basic block was, after all, the same one we had used since the beginning whenever we had needed a new hospital, headquarters, control center or school. The basic block was the Wehrmacht barrack — those mass-produced German military buildings which were so exactly alike in façade and floor plan that you could go from end to end of Germany and find your way about in any casern-type DP camp or in any blockhouse within that camp, knowing unerringly, for example, that room 204 was three doors removed from the washroom on the second floor and that it was a five-family room with four windows along one wall. Although the long middle hallway traversing the Resettlement Center appeared at first glance as provocative as a corridor through Cook's, with neat signs angling out from the repainted doors naming the mission within — CANADA, BELGIUM, UNITED KINGDOM, FRANCE, AUSTRALIA, SOUTH AMERICA — you nevertheless relived your same old emotions when you stood in the hallway with hand on doorknob, half expecting to walk into a blanket-celled honeycomb crowded with murmuring DP's. And even after you did walk in to greet the Canadian or Australian official sitting there, you were always faintly surprised not to see diapers drying on a line stretched above his immaculate desk.

The DP's also had this sense of deep familiarity with the new setting. They scurried through the Center like knowledgeable rabbits, never pausing to ask the way to room 202. Sometimes you saw them gazing around the Resettlement Center rooms as if the walls were talking to them. Ignatz refused to be downcast by my continuing failure to locate in Chicago a certain John Smith named Basyli Sikorski, because in our Resettlement Center the room reserved for the United States Consul was the facsimile of the blockhouse room in Wildflecken where his first son had been born. He took this as a good omen, deriving comfort from his mystical spatial relationship with the unknown *grosse Fische* who would one day walk into that room with the great visa seal of the United States in a diplomatic pouch which would be set down, *vielleicht,* right there where Stanislaw's cradle had stood.

Enterprising DP's from all the Würzburg area camps had already snatched up the concessions which Londa, as chief welfare, was supposed to allocate impartially to her most deserving camp businessmen and I observed, with a twinge of pride because they were my first love, that the Poles from Wildflecken had cornered the two most profitable concessions, hairdressing and passport photos, posting their shop signs diplomatically in German — *Damen u. Herren Friseur* and *Fotograf* — so as to attract all the nationalities that eventually would be swarming through that place of final exit.

From its first days when only the emigrants for Canada, Australia and the Argentine were passing through it, the Resettlement Center was as exciting as Grand Central Terminal, with an atmosphere totally opposite to the camps it resembled physically. Here every face had that going-away look and everybody was clad in his Sunday best. The loud-speakers attached to tall poles throughout the Center called out in all languages a continuing stream of orders to report — to Medical, to Security, to Baggage Rooms or to the grouping point in garage No. 3 where another contingent was loading for the train to Bremerhaven and the ship to Australia and even though the loud-speaker always began with *Achtung! Achtung!* nobody listened to it with the fright of old associations. The DP's lifted their faces eagerly to its blare, each one hoping to hear his name on the roll call. As the Dombrowskis, the Kowalskis, the Artemowiczes and the Jankaukases dropped from the high horns, the owners of the names were instantly apparent, emerging from the YMCA canteen, the reading rooms and lecture halls and heading in purposeful beelines toward the doorway of the mission building.

Even the DP's employed in the Resettlement Center, mainly workers who for various reasons (such as a spot on the lung or a marital situation to be cleared up) would not be presentable to any mission for quite some time, were alight as they never had been in the camps, where we had known them only in the gray tones of routine and resignation. I had to look twice before recognizing Madame Stanislawa from Wildflecken, now interpreter to the IRO Resettlement Center director, with her close-cropped hair coifed by the Center *friseur* and her Wehrmacht ski pants replaced by a Bavarian peasant skirt that swung in slow lovely rhythm as she walked toward me revealing, for the first time, the way she could smile. I saw again the bitter battle of the Red Cross warehouse and the frozen red hands of her PW women as her changeless husky voice recited the current events in the lives of her Magdalenes, many of whom had followed her to the Resettlement Center to work as charwomen and potato-peelers while waiting with her for the DP Act to be passed so they could start moving toward the farm co-operative in Illinois which had promised to sponsor them all.

Stanislawa had leapt at the opportunity of employment in the Resettlement Center because it brought her closer to the sources of power. She had studied the idiosyncrasies of the mission men as if reading one of those small-scale maps of a combat terrain and had already observed that late afternoon (just about the time the Army-controlled bar in the officers' club was opening for the day) was the most favorable time to have an emigration interview, that well-groomed applicants got through the initial encounter faster than the slovenly ones, and that delay of the DP after call-forward was more irritating to the Canadian than to the Australian officials.

"Doubtless because of the more frequent ships to Canada," she said. "But all this I make for reconnaissance only, for that great day when your country will start to call forward. It is well to know, as you say, the ropes."

Call forward, in processing, final shipment... the new language of the Resettlement Center was exciting to hear, a functional phrasing descriptive of the production-line stages of that great emigration mill which changed the faces of everyone who entered it and the fates of everyone who got through it.

I knew that my first visit had changed me. I had a new center of gravity. Henceforth, "from now on out" as we said colloquially, the Resettlement Center would be the focal point toward which every thought would turn. The camps were gruesome to return to after a visit to the wildly humming Resettlement Center, as if you had stepped from light into shadow, flash-backed from a moving finale to some early chapter in the narrative which did not require repetition. Even though the planes of the airlift were now droning overhead above the summer river fogs that enveloped Aschaffenburg and most of our DP's were sleeping with some quick-to-snatch parcel under their beds containing the essentials for hasty flight, we could no longer feel an emotion for this new hazard. We received the anxious delegations from the camps with something like irritation because we had done all this before. Go back to your camps and sit tight, we said, there is no danger. And the clipped bold words of Churchill in Missouri were answered by the growl of Stalin in Moscow and all this was happening in Wildflecken two years ago when we had had our first baptism in DP fears and had worn masks of pretense because we were two lifetimes younger then and could feel freshly about each new experiencing.

"This all seems like something in parentheses," said Londa.

It was true. With our new center of gravity in the Resettlement Center, our camp days under the airlift felt like a repetitive phrasing in parentheses. The steady drone of the planes was almost soporific in continuity except when we used it as background copy in the letters we were still writing to potential sponsors overseas in

America; then we listened to it and thought how to bring that threatening sound into some farmhouse out on the Kansas prairies, into the ears of some farmer who might be needing hired hands to help with the harvest.

I thought I could never again be moved by anything that happened in the camps... or over them. I trudged through my workdays in them like a rat on a wheel, never expecting anything new or different until after the DP Act would be passed, which would give us another wheel to work on.

And then the Jews came.

We had never had a Jewish camp in our northern area and had been slightly patronized by team members from the Jewish camps around Munich for this blind spot in our DP experience, as if our two years with Poles, Balts and Ukrainians counted for little.

"You haven't entered into the spirit of the thing till you've tried to run a Jewish camp," they said. "Wildflecken? *Pfui!* Not even rehearsal."

The Jews numbered less than one fifth of our Zone's total DP population but they were such an articulate minority that if you only read the newspapers to learn about Occupation affairs, you gained the impression that they were the whole of the DP problem. They made the headlines regularly, especially when their camps were cited for closing. They would stage hunger strikes in protest and frighten the wits out of Army and IRO by their wailing and wasting away. You had to handle them with kid gloves, it was said, especially when transferring them from one camp to another, and heaven help the IRO worker who left a loop of barbed wire visible in any camp to which they were to be transferred. They were classified "persecutees" — the only DP's except medical cases who got a special food ration because of a nonworker status. They sounded like the prima donnas of the DP world, but I thought that perhaps they deserved the rating. I knew that some of those Jews had survived the last stand in the Warsaw ghetto and that a great many of them who had survived the concentration-camp ovens had lived like hunted animals until the liberation. Despite their apocryphal publicity, it stood to reason that they could not be more than the ashes of a people and I waited for them with mingled emotions of alarm and compassion.

For days prior to our scheduled reception of seventeen hundred Jewish DP's from a camp over near the Czech border, we received their inspecting delegations. They were not the ashes of a people at all. They were charged with the intensest life force I had ever experienced. From the moment of my first encounter with their contrary, critical and demanding leaders, I had the feeling that I was dealing not with people but with phoenixes. The wild way they used up their energies, which their thin wiry bodies seemed incapable of generating in the first place, was alarming to behold. Their smoldering eyes looked like burnt holes but they missed absolutely nothing, as if the flames that had passed through them had only sharpened their sight. Their voices were unmusical and hoarse from violent expostulation and their hands moved continuously in manual dialogue of a derisory nature. They didn't seem like DP's at all. "We Jews..." they said, and it was like hearing ancestral portraits speak. You wondered if they even bothered to carry DP identity cards as they passed through this phase of their centuries-old displacement.

We showed off the big camp we were making ready for them, like rental agents proud of an accommodation that was, without doubt, the handsomest DP housing in all Bavaria. It was a whole air base near Würzburg, built originally to house Goering's kingly Luftwaffe and just recently vacated by American air-force officers and their wives. The Jewish delegates viewed the neat small officers' houses with gardens and white picket fences around, the creamy woodwork and rose-tinted walls inside, the varnished stairways and windows opening out on fresh vistas of farmland. The rabbis shook their heads. It didn't seem to be good enough. They talked all the time among themselves in excitable Yiddish that had a sound of liking what they saw, but when they addressed us in German, it was only to point out defects. Only one kitchen for every four apartments?... It would make bad blood among their housewives.

"But American housewives got along peaceably," we said.

"We Jews..." Their hands flew around almost faster than the eye could follow.

We led them to the other half of the air-base camp where enlisted men's blockhouses stood in rows around a central plaza. We told them like conspirators that the IRO engineers had even appropriated materials from the sacred reserves of the Resettlement Center to patch up broken windows and restore pilfered light sockets. They inspected the setting that could house some two thousand and shook their heads more vigorously. Fifteen hundred could never squeeze in here, they said. And as for those mess kitchens (with rows of gleaming fifty-gallon cookers in perfect repair), they would never be adequate to prepare the kosher foods for their special groups. Walking from building to building, the rabbis kept glancing over the rich farm valley that held the air base as in a shallow saucer rimmed prettily in places with blackthorn hedges in snowy bloom. I thought they were approving their healthy pastoral surroundings until one of them said mournfully, "It is lonely here. No big cities."

There was a small German community set down on the highway that divided the two halves of the camp. The delegates talked excitedly as they looked at the beer hall, the rural police and bus stations and the stone farmhouses clustered around. Maybe, I thought, they accept this in lieu of a city; but when they came out of their energy-burning huddle, they said that this was the most dangerous feature of all; the IRO must agree to arm their Jewish police to protect their people from these Germans living in their midst. A few Germans were standing about listening to the explosive Yiddish and looking more ready to ask protection from the coming invasion than to attack it. That nearly every German in that village would be cheerfully in the employ of the Jews within a fortnight after their arrival never even entered my head as I soothingly promised to plead for authorization to arm a DP police. Anything to assure a smooth move without incident, Sam had said, anything short of the moon...

They bade us farewell with a strange old-world courtesy, saying that perhaps our air-base camp would do for the short time they would be in it. Soon they would be starting the emigration to Israel so what matter what kind of camp we offered? Fire leaped from their burnt-out eyes when they said the word. *Ees-rye-yel, Ees-rye-yel!* It was startling to hear a sound of music from those raw scrawny throats.

We watched them drive away in a small fleet of battered sedans, obviously the result of some fast trading with the Germans. Our transport officer, whose duty it was to impound every private car owned by DP's, gazed with frank admiration at the parade of forbidden vehicles and said, "They even organize Army gas for those jalopies."

"They're bringing in an entire clothing factory!" said Londa. "And d'ye know, I'm asked to requisition that empty hall in the German section for their school. They don't want our DP nurses. They run their own medical show, they said. They don't even need penicillin from us!"

It seemed as if we were all talking faster than usual, as if contact with those rabbis robed in rusty black had somehow rejuvenated us.

I couldn't find any familiar words to describe what I had felt about the Jewish DP's. I only knew that I had been on the begging end of the negotiations all the way through, that it was a pleasurable new experience in my DP work and that I had been arguing, not with ordinary people, but with something almost abstract and transcendental, like a phoenix or a naked idea.

All seventeen hundred Jews came to us on a rainy day in mid-May, in bulging boxcars that stretched seemingly for miles back of the bombed airplane hangars where the railroad siding was. We had paced off the difficult unloading terrain and the siding that held only six or eight cars at a time. We had beaten into the heads of our DP truck drivers the stiff Army order to keep off the mile-long cement runways that crisscrossed the airfield and offered multiple-choice direct routes to the camp. We had led the drivers over the bumpy road that passed around the airfield's edge and through a barricaded gate and had shown them the guardhouse where the Jewish billeting master would sit and hand out to each incoming individual a slip naming blockhouse and room number. That way, our Jewish delegation had said, there could be no argument. It looked like the most beautifully organized reception that had ever been plotted on paper.

The Jewish DP police in woolly green tunics, with the Star of David on their caps, were the first to leap from the boxcars. They thrust aside Georgi's specially selected Balt and Ukrainian police and took up battle stations along the tracks. The gentry destined for the officers' section of the camp would descend first. The billeting master turned out to be a woman named Rachel, a compact bundle of energy with red cheeks and snapping black eyes who could outshout the Jewish police and the clothing-factory men who wanted to put their valuable machinery first into the waiting trucks. Our unloading plan seemed to fall to pieces in the pandemonium. Across the forbidden airstrips of the flying field, the first of our DP truck drivers to have been bribed by eager householders (out of sight of Rachel's commanding eyes) were piloting heaped-high trucks like crazy barnstormers, with our transport officer jeeping after them in hot pursuit. In the din of wild hoarse shouting, of crates thumping to the ground, of trucks roaring off without orders and violent quarrels going on in any place where two or more people were gathered, you couldn't think of anything to do except to follow the nearest moving object and hope that it would lead you somehow out of the chaos.

I followed Rachel to the room-assignment office in the guardhouse down by the airfield gate, whose red-and-white barricade was now but a splintered stump recording some swift passage through it. I watched her lay out her listing of seventeen hundred names, each with an explicit room number appended. Already, by my calculation of the renegade trucks, at least three hundred people had captured the rooms with views in the officers' section of the camp. I wondered how she would ever come out of it. I didn't know (until weeks afterwards) that I was watching one of the few women who had crawled out of the deathtrap of the

Warsaw ghetto through the flooded sewers that led to the Aryan side, carrying a packet of priceless ammunition above her head, above the fetid waters that shelved her chin on slime. What she had to come out of now was child's play.

By the time the first legally loaded trucks appeared at the guardhouse, the first illegal squatters were back from the officers' billets demanding assignment to the room numbers Rachel was handing out calmly to the people in the trucks. I could only deduce that she told them to fight it out among themselves because that was what they promptly proceeded to do. Yiddish splattered around hot as machine-gun fire. The light May rain seemed to evaporate in the murderous heat above the trucks where bits of numbered paper were shaken in faces purple with rage. If you shut your eyes, you had the impression that people were being beaten, racked and throttled. I cowered in the guardhouse beside Rachel.

"Such a people," she said scornfully. "I am ashamed that you should see." She pounded her brown fist down on hands reaching through the window and cried *"Ach!"* as one exclaims when killing flies. She saved her real voice until the crowd began to invade her tiny office to read the billeting list over her shoulder; then her stream of Yiddish caught them like a fire hose, dashing them out the door and back into their trucks to await their turns in proper sequence.

"You would not think we have organization," she said between blasts at the clamoring throng. But I was already beginning to see the shape of order in that seeming chaos as truck after truck howled and shouted its way past the guardhouse and on toward the camp, an entire population turning about the single powerful young matriarch who had the final word in every dispute and laid it down like Law. She could do this because every room had been assigned with plan and foresight weeks before the move, when their welfare committees had sat over the air-base floor plans and had matched families to rooms with a thoroughness that left no ground for argument since children got southern exposures, old people the first-floor spaces, and doctors, rabbis and chiefs of all the turbulent camp activities the quieter cottages of the officers' section.

Nothing had been left to chance or last-minute improvisation, although everything looked as if it had. The superbly organized Jews ran their own show the way they wanted it — fast, efficient and tumultuous as an incoming tide, a tide that brought us not only seventeen hundred people with dark broody eyes and imperishable vocal cords, but also the driving spirit that animated them all, a passionate nationalism for a country that had just been born and was still a bitter battleground.

Israel! Zion! The tensions and strife of that bony bridge of land did not seem thousands of miles distant in Palestine. Each day's developments were re-enacted right there in the air-base camp in the middle of rural Bavaria. Military Government warned us that our Jews must be quiet and behave like other DP's until the proper time came when it would be safe to allow them to emigrate to their new homeland. The way the Jews looked at us when we tried to explain the humanitarian idea of not repatriating people to a battleground made us feel as if we were talking rubbish. Rachel's welfare office was hung with martial posters depicting young Jewish girls in trenches hurling grenades at Arabs. The Jewish DP police practiced marksmanship with the carbines we had secured for them — as "defense" against the Germans who were now gainfully employed in the heavy manual labor of the camp. The Jewish workshops swung into swift production of fine woolen greatcoats and stout leather shoes heavily hobnailed for rough terrain. We could only guess that this too was all for Israel and, through some mysterious channels, was ultimately delivered there. We never saw any of our Jewish DP's wearing the useful clothing.

The dynamic drive of our new DP's to get some place other than the U.S.A. was such a reversal, after our years of door-watching with other DP's, that we ceased for a time to think of those others or even of the Resettlement Center that had been our final focal emotion. Each day we hurried to the air-base camp, half expecting to find that it had blown up with the force of its own internal combustion since we had left it seething the night before. Each of us had specific jobs to do in the "settling in" of the new camp but we all felt like fifth wheels on a wagon hitched to a comet. All sorts of organizations swarmed in to take care of their own people. The Jewish Agency for Palestine handled the enrollments for Israel. The American ORT set up machinery workshops and taught schoolboys, who stood no taller than gnomes before the big forges, to turn out fine precision tools; mechanics were needed in Israel. The American Joint Distribution Committee brought in raw materials for clothing and cobbler shops and special food reinforcements to the IRO ration to build back, we concluded, some of the mass energy burnt up daily in the excited never-ending talk about Israel. Over all the ferment and frenzy flapped a flag we had never seen before, a delicate ethereal flag of pale blue stripes on a white ground with the Star of David stitched in narrow blue bands in the center of the field. It was an age-old dream coming to life under our eyes, but we could not realize that until long afterwards.

Possibly we never would have been able to tear ourselves away from the engrossing drama of the Jewish camp if "Operation Bird Dog" had not been suddenly announced. Sam had mysteriously prepared his team supervisors for some momentous news and had ordered us to go back to Aschaffenburg and to stick by the telephones there, no matter what hell might be breaking loose elsewhere in the area.

Near midnight on the fifteenth of June, 1948, he blitz-called us to announce that Operation Bird Dog was in effect. This was the most closely guarded secret of the U.S. Zone and the only one, to my knowledge, that the DP's did not know about in advance. It was the great overnight currency reform which was to set Western Germany on its financial feet, wipe out the old reichsmark, which had less value than second-hand wallpaper and institute the Deutsche Mark, valued roughly at 4.2 to the dollar, almost at par with the solid Swiss franc. Within the next forty-eight hours, Sam said, every inhabitant in the land, including our DP's, would be permitted to exchange up to forty reichsmarks on a one-to-one basis for the new Deutsche Marks which had been printed nine months earlier by the U.S. Treasury Department in the darkest secrecy of its deepest vaults.

It was as exciting as receiving another Jewish camp. At dawn next day I drove over the mountains to pick up from Military Post in Würzburg sacks of the crisp new currency to pay off our six thousand DP's in the Aschaffenburg area. Every IRO worker, including this time our doctors and nurses, was assigned to the control and supervision of the gigantic money exchange and it was not until it was over and we had totted up our accounts that we realized that we, in our small corner of the DP world, had handled more than sixty thousand dollars in that day's unprecedented activities. We doubted that every one of our DP's would have forty reichsmarks in his pocket and innocently planned on having to return some of the money to Military Post, which all went to show how little we knew about the people we had lived among for three years. Not a DP turned up at the counting tables with a pfennig less than the maximum allowance for exchange! *Forty DM's to every DP* had shot over the camp grapevines even as we set out our carefully audited nominal rolls and bundles of Deutsche Marks. Beggarly old grannies and orphan children were courted in every camp and persuaded to utilize their individual exchange privileges to help the clubs, committees and plutocrats realize the maximum possible on their now worthless reichsmark reserves... for a consideration, of course, a percentage of the take to the penniless ones who had a right but no cash to exercise it with. It was without doubt the greatest share-the-wealth program ever launched by a resourceful people (for a few hours only) and there must have been a triple-entry bookkeeping astronomical in complication behind the long lines of DP's queued up at the exchange desks, many of them obviously fumbling the first reichsmarks they had ever held in their shaking hands. But it was all within the law. Every DP who lived and breathed was entitled to Deutsche Marks up to forty if he presented himself with the equivalent in reichsmarks. Families with masses of children were looked at with envy for the first time since the selective emigration programs had begun. Toddlers and babes in arms had the same exchange right as the adults — there was no age limit on this magnificent windfall. Men who had wives in Chouka's maternity hospital made hourly visits to see if their little women were in labor yet and, she suspected, even jounced their spouses around a bit to add, if possible, one more member to their families before nightfall when the currency exchange would end. And, indeed, toward the zero hour, when our fingers were numbed from careful counting, we occasionally heard feet running down the hallway and a crazy wild shouting as some frantic father burst into the guarded pay-room waving a brand-new birth certificate.

When his DP friends got through clapping him on the back, kissing him on both cheeks and hugging him like a winner in a race against time, we paid out the forty Deutsche Marks to which his five-minute-old baby was entitled.

It was small wonder that with days like that and the fearful accounting that followed (matching a DP signature, X mark or thumbprint against each forty of the quarter-million Deutsche Marks we had handed out) not a single one of us in the field was aware that the DP Act had been passed by Congress on June 25 and that when we did hear about it some days later from our own DP's, we paid no attention to the idiotic rumor.

~ 15 ~

It was called Public Law 774 and it was passed in the second session of the Eightieth Congress.

Over the whole of the DP world an unnatural quiet settled, as if our refugees had decided en masse to lie low and behave with exemplary decorum until the IRO would publish a simplified version of the DP Act and tell each what his chances were of being included in the two hundred and two thousand whom the United States would admit within the next two years. We had no noteworthy problems or incidents in that summer and fall of '48 while the vast machinery for the implementation of a law was being set up — the mill of the gods visible there before our eyes.

At first, all that we in the field knew about the DP Act was what we read in the newspapers. It was some months before working copies reached us. By that time, such sheaves of interpretive directives had come down from our higher headquarters, such delegations of authority and definitions of terms, that we were taken aback by the compact brevity of the original Act — a mouse-sized document compared to the leviathan our own organization had labored over and brought forth. This was my first working acquaintance with a public law. In my naïveté I had thought it would read something like what was graven at the base of the Statue of Liberty... "Give me your tired, your poor, Your huddled masses yearning to breathe free, The wretched refuse of your teeming shore..." But the lady who lifted the lamp beside the golden door did not write the DP Act. You had to read between the dots of every Congressional colon, beneath the tail of every comma. Sinister meanings could be concealed in a *notwithstanding* or a *therefore,* like traps set among fine flowers of verbiage.

The traps, which newspapers called "discriminatory clauses in the new law," all had faces and names for us. They were set for the people with whom we had lived and worked for three years. The allocation of two hundred and two thousand visas, for example, specified forty per cent to DP's "whose place of origin or country of nationality has been *de facto* annexed by a foreign power." When you penetrated that *de facto* and realized that it meant that almost half the total visas were reserved for Balts, you saw many of your Poles, the great majority of your DP world, possibly shut out because their country had not been *de facto* annexed, but only secretly stolen. Then there was the trap we called the "farmer clause" — thirty per cent of all visas must be given to persons who had been "previously engaged in agricultural pursuits." Worriedly you thought of your DP doctors, nurses, professors and engineers; would the bortsch gardens they cultivated back of their blockhouses count as agricultural pursuits? DP's who had blood relatives in the States were placed only third on the priority list, which put Ignatz's Uncle Basyli, now excitedly writing from Chicago that he had filed an assurance and leased a small house, possibly far down on the waiting list.

"But it's that entry dateline that worries me most," said Londa. From her welfare counseling, she knew many DP's who would be caught in that trap.

The law specified that to be eligible under the DP Act, a displaced person must have entered one of the Western Zones on or after September 1, 1939 (date of Hitler's blitz into Poland), or on or before December 22, 1945. This dateline bracket excluded all late-comers from Iron Curtain countries, such as the Czechs who did not start coming over until late '47. It shut out likewise all the early comers, many of whom, like workingmen anywhere in the world, had followed the trek toward higher wages which in early '39 were being paid only in Nazi Germany. And who could say if those migrant workers had realized that the cement they were pouring was for the dragon teeth of the Siegfried Line, for the reinforced cradles of the submarine pens? You could feel anguish building up as you realized that that date of entry into Germany would divide the sheep from the goats, the meek who had waited for Hitler to blitz in and take them from the self-reliant who conceivably could have read the writing on the wall and reported to work inside Germany ahead of the conscripted labor while real wages were still being paid.

The same list we had used to divide our forcibly displaced from our voluntarily displaced was going to be the instrument the DP Act would use — the fearsome and irrevocable EWZ list. This was the *Einwanderungszentrale,* the complete immigration files of Nazi Germany, containing the vital statistics on every foreigner who had applied for immigration into the Fatherland — his name, age, place of origin, date of entry and two photographs of him, full face and profile. When the Allies captured that great archive intact, they captured the key to the cross-word puzzle of the DP world. We knew how efficient were those Nazi immigration files; we had already used them to screen from the camps all those who had entered Germany before Hitler's blitz into their homelands. Helmut, my Estonian baron, was one of these. He had come into Germany in late August of 1939, a few days' difference in time from that specified in the DP Act, which was going to cost him his opportunity to emigrate to the U.S.A. But his three maiden aunts, who had not fled Estonia until the Russians occupied it in June 1940, would be eligible under the Act.

Thus it was that when we studied the Act and looked at our DP's through the eyes of the law, our Stanislawas, Helmuts and Ignatzes were transformed into datelines, required skills and nationality preferences. Initial rejoicing over the Act turned to foreboding as we realized that that was how the enforcing agencies would see our refugees — the Displaced Persons Commission men who would select the eligibles, the U.S. Public Health doctors who would give the bill of health, and the Immigration Service officers who would interrogate them before final clearance. As scores of these power-possessing individuals began coming into the field with their law books, visa seals and X-ray eyes, we trembled like our DP's who would have to run that gamut of investigators, any one of whom could knock you out of the running with the painless tap on your back of a wrong dateline or a lung shadow.

The only people who seemed to be on our side were the familiar voluntary agency representatives, many of whom had been in the field since the early days and knew our DP's almost as well as we did. They were to come into the field in vastly greater numbers now, each agency armed with assurances of jobs and housing in the States which their church and synagogue groups at home had pledged. Even if a DP had no friend or relative to sponsor him for the States, he still had a good chance of getting there on one of these unnamed assurances from his own religious group which were to be matched up for job requirement and named in the field. The Lutheran World Federation would cover the Lutheran DP's, Church World Service the Protestant and Orthodox, National Catholic Welfare Conference the Roman Catholics, Hebrew Immigrant Aid Society and AJDC the Jews, and so on down through all the separate faiths that had got together, long before the DP Act was passed, and stirred up sympathy and support for the DP's just as our voyaging Baptist pastor had predicted in the desolate door-watching summer of 1947.

The voluntary agency people swarmed into the field with thousands of unnamed assurances and began the greatest matching operation ever seen in human affairs — a veritable man-hunt to find in the flesh the exact type of worker described on each affidavit, with a family of specified size that would fit into the house or rooms held in readiness. At last we could see the usefulness of the exhaustive studies we had done on our DP — mountains of descriptive paper beneath which we thought we had buried him. Under the main categories of nationality, age, skill, creed and family composition, we had him "broken down" practically to color of eyes, so that if any voluntary agency wanted, say, fifty blue-eyed Balts in a hurry, each with a family of no more than six and no dependents over sixty-five years of age, we could produce the people from our statistical Himalayas in nothing flat.

You want a Lithuanian skilled in violin repair? We have him. You want a hundred tractor drivers? We have them. Fifty Poles for work in the tobacco fields? We have five thousand. A neat clean old lady agile enough to be an invalid's companion? Here she is. We had everything the employer-citizens of the States were asking for and thousands more besides.

A Lutheran representative showed me my first actual assurance — a piece of paper in search of a person. Everything was written into it except the name of the DP it would eventually cover. The sponsor was a Scandinavian farmer in the Midwest who had five hundred acres with no mortgage, a guesthouse (with running water) that could accommodate a family of four, preference Balts, for farm work with all modern equipment. It moved me strangely to read the name of a private citizen who had gone to all the trouble of filing, through the DP Commission in Washington, an affidavit of support for an unknown family of foreigners overseas. It seemed such a risky thing for that farmer to have done. It made my head spin to think that some hundred thousand of my fellow citizens were doing the same thing, offering to take into their homes, sight unseen in most cases, an alien family speaking an outlandish tongue, with maybe a dictatorial pipe-smoking grandmother included in the lot or one of those strange small children who had been born in a DP camp and could not imagine or desire any other life. What were they thinking of, all those risky reachers into the grab bag of our DP world? When I tried to imagine their faces — foresighted, practical and possibly covetous for a fresh stock of skilled labor, all I could see was the pure visage of Charity.

The match-up task was terrific in scope since about ninety per cent of the assurances under the Act came through the denominational agencies, unnamed. We in IRO went about with our pockets stuffed with capsule case histories of favorite DP's which we handed out like bonbons to the fagged agency people roaming the camps. Each time a new block of assurances was received from Washington, through the DP Commission clearing center in Frankfurt, and forwarded to the field for matching, we gathered like flies around the receiving agency, buzzing with helpful suggestions. I found that I could even stoop to fawn, if need be, when I knew that an agency worker had assurances from California calling for workers in the orange groves. Such an invitation to Eden almost made me regret Ignatz's "nominated assurance" which came from Chicago through the devious control channels with his name already inscribed upon it. But Ignatz was not wistfully weighing an orange grove against the Polish section of Chicago. He was busy as a bird dog completing his vast documentation for presentation to the DP Commission in our local Resettlement Center. What with birth and marriage certificates, good-conduct statements from the police, work-testing records proving he was skilled in the mechanical work his uncle offered and even a weird little document called "nonbegging certificate" which could be secured only from German authorities (proving you had not begged during your sojourn in Germany), he had to have a little of the bird dog instinct to track down all the documents required under the law.

Helping him with his homework, I learned the routine of this second step in the slow milling process that would eventually land a DP in the States. Two weeks after a DP received his European Case Number (which Frankfurt DP Commission gave to each assurance as soon as it was named) he was supposed to have completed his documentation. Since Ignatz's birth certificate had shown his origin east of the River Bug, he had prudently destroyed it in one of our times of tension when it had looked as if the Russians would beat the U.S. DP Commission into the Zone. But his village priest, who had baptized him in Poland, used to live in Wildflecken, Ignatz said. Would a word from him be acceptable? It took me two days to find out that a sworn statement from a reputable authority would be acceptable in lieu of a birth certificate and it took Ignatz one week to locate the elderly priest practically on his deathbed in an IRO TB sanitarium at the other end of the Zone. Ignatz completed his documentation in three weeks, with the help of two resettlement officers, a chief welfare and my personal car, which I lent to him for fast tracking of the moribund priest. I wondered what other DP's (who were not so heavily dowered with official affection) were doing about their paper work, especially the ones who had taken ten minutes just to sign their names in receipt of their forty Deutsche Marks in the recent currency exchange.

"It's quite simple," said Londa. "We do it for them."

Our chief resettlement officer, who had a peculiar Swedish sense of humor, measured the documents in a single case file and found that they stretched out end to end for a distance of seventeen yards.

Step three was the presenting of these seventeen yards of paper to the local DP Commission, now handsomely installed in our Resettlement Center with a floor all to themselves. By the time Ignatz's documents were presented, thousands of other DP's had also got theirs in, so that the commission offices resembled some great paper mill and the men running that part of the show had the frazzled Federal-agency faces of people who fight paper all their lives. It startled me to learn that none of them would see a DP (except through the popeyed photograph included in his documents) until the very last moment when he would be called forward and presented to the consul for visa. The DP Commission "selectors" read the DP's case file and determined his eligibility from the paper he had presented. The law, which they were appointed to uphold, was not interested in the look of the DP behind the paper, in the way he held his head or hung it. Nobody but the consul at the far end of the production line would see those slow Slavic smiles that won the heart.

The case files were each ticked with a small colored tab which told where the case was at that moment — red tabs for security investigation by CIC (Counter-Intelligence Corps), green tabs for medical deferrals, white tabs for "required document missing," and so on through the rainbow of reasons why a DP must wait to be called forward for his final days in the Center before shipment out. The initial estimate on time required to process a DP through to final shipment was four months from the time he received his European Case Number. I expressed surprise that it could take so long, recalling the pristine simplicity of the Belgian mission that had looked at a DP, listened to his heart and sent him forward to the coal mines with a pat on the back, all in a few days of time.

"But we have a law to uphold," said the commission man who was showing me around their shop. "These people, you know. You can't be too careful." He glanced out the window at the happy called-forward DP's babbling and gesticulating in the plaza below. His face was earnest and thoughtful, like faces sometimes seen in a zoo staring through a pane of glass at something furred or feathered.

"So much can happen to a DP family in four months," I said. "All sorts of things to delay their processing." Births, deaths, measles, lung spots, denunciations from jealous neighbors — I could think of a hundred hazards in the time it took to say "delay." Even death of the patiently waiting sponsor overseas, which would necessitate finding a new one and doing several of the seventeen yards of paper all over again. Yes, that could happen too.

But, in those halcyon days when the great U.S. program was grinding to a start and DP's were actually getting through in four months' time, not one of us could imagine, as we hovered worriedly over our active case loads, that when the first year of the two-year program would be completed, the word "delay" would have spawned a hundred new meanings and that the DP's processing time would have stretched out to six, then eight months, with not a few classic cases, like Ignatz's, dragging through the mill for more than a year. By June 1950, when Congress would take pity on us and extend the DP Act for another year, you wouldn't be able to say who looked more like Laocoön — the DP family or us trying to extricate it from the multiple loops of a law.

Despite the pitfalls in the U.S. scheme visible to all, so many DP'S wanted to switch to it from their processing for sure bets like Belgium, Australia and Canada that we began to publicize letters from satisfied customers in those countries to take the mass mind off the gold-paved streets of Neuyorke Amerika. When I posted the letters on the bulletin boards, it was like tacking up live tissue that spoke and smiled and beckoned...

Good day my wife Sinaida and my son Vitalij — Yesterday at 3 o'clock we arrived to Belgium. In our group are 15 men. On the Belgian frontier we were met by music and the Red Cross very well and gifted by oranges, cakes and coffee. In the restaurant we received the meal of the soup with meat and macaronis, of cutlet (100 grams) and of 1 bottle good beer. I will try describe what I saw in the town, but you will not believe me. I have not seen till now such a life, you can buy all what you want — Bacon 60 Fr., Sugar 25 Fr., Oranges 8 Fr. and you may buy these things without limit. The same in relation to clothes. We shall work in the mine 700 meters deep but there is no danger. The day wages are from 147 to 250 Fr. I work that you be brought here as soon as possible. Everything will be all right for us here. Patience, my wife, you shall soon live as the human beings...

In that first summer of the U.S. scheme, we were innocently unaware of another law which had to be fulfilled even after everybody (DP Commission, U.S. Public Health and U.S. Consul) had put the seal of acceptance on the papers and their owners whom we joyously bundled into the trains for Bremen. This other law was no mouse-sized document. It was called *Immigration and Nationality Laws and Regulations* and it filled a book as thick as Walt Whitman's *Leaves of Grass,* with print that was very much smaller and no breathing space between the lines. The immigration laws lay in wait for the emigrating DP at the very end of his long pilgrim's progress toward the gangplank of a ship. A section of the U.S. Immigration and Naturalization Service had been transferred from Ellis Island to the port of Bremen and, like a thorn among roses, was set up in IRO's splendid embarkation center located there.

We all knew of course about the Immigration and Naturalization Service, but not one of us in the field had ever seen the book of the laws it enforced. We thought familiarly of the I & NS officers. Many of us in prewar days had submitted our passports to their gimlet-eyed inspectors upon return to the States from vacations abroad. That their final interrogation of our visaed DP's could turn out to be the most fateful trap of all never even occurred to us until we began to receive frantic letters from favorites detained in Bremen by the Immigration Service that had found something wrong in their seventeen yards of paper, or in some member of their families or even, occasionally, in the magic carpet of their visas which a consul down in the areas might have forgotten to sign. Time was required to clarify each detained case and there was no time. Within four months after issuance, a visa expired, and if the emigrant had not set foot on American soil by then, or on the deck of an IRO ship which counted as American soil, then he had to go back to the camps and wait until possibly the end of the program when something called "a replacement visa" would be issued.

My first intimation of the wheels within wheels of the immigration law came in the spring of 1949 when I was furiously hawking about to find a new sponsor for Ignatz, whose Uncle Basyli had been killed in the traffic of the Chicago Loop, thereby canceling automatically the named assurance on which Ignatz had processed practically up to consular visa. Ordinarily, the Catholic agency would have clapped one of their unnamed assurances on the case and Ignatz could have proceeded smoothly onward to visa. But I discovered to my dismay that his was a "mixed marriage" — he a Catholic, his wife not — so there had to be dickering between agency and sponsor overseas to see if such a family would be acceptable. Meanwhile, Londa received a letter from her welfare counterpart in Bremen, telling that another of our old-time favorites was in trouble. The Immigration Service had excluded one of Stanislawa's PW women on the charge of "moral turpitude," a ground for exclusion on a par with idiocy, contagious diseases and illiteracy.

"You remember her," Londa said. "Lubja, the little black-eyed one who could outwrestle the Polish guard." I read the letter with sinking heart. Apparently an enamored guardsman, seeking to delay Lubja until his own case was ready for final shipment, had written a love letter of entreaty to the Immigration Service which interpreted the passion as moral turpitude. Stanislawa and her remaining PW women refused to sail without Lubja; their visas were expiring. The Bremen Welfare would of course appeal Lubja's case, as was permissible under immigration law, but it might take months to assemble the testimony. Would Londa please forward some background material on early days in Wildflecken? And how would she advise counseling that stern chieftain to sail without one of the brood to which she seemed so fanatically devoted?

"I'll write to Stanislawa myself," Londa said. "That Bremen Welfare is good, but I think it takes a voice from the old Red Cross warehouse this time."

Case by case we fought to free the caught ones, working hand in glove with the agencies whose assurances had paved the way. Almost every day someone discovered something new about the DP Act, until it seemed that every restrictive phrase had a hundred faces — like "firmly resettled," in which we saw all the ghostlike returnees from repatriation to Poland and all the brave young men who had gone off to Belgium and, having honorably completed their coal-mining contract, had returned to the Zone to get aboard the band wagon for the States. Ineligible under the Act were these "firmly resettled" ones, the persons who had voluntarily emigrated or repatriated to a country outside the DP world. Only the Jews, who could claim and prove persecution in any Eastern European country in which they had set foot, could get out of that trap. But not Tak Tak Schön and others like him who had fled only the smell of danger before that danger had turned into a personal and provable persecution. The DP Act was like a juggernaut that both carried and crushed. By the spring of '49 it had carried some twenty thousand DP's to the States, which from our toilsome send-off point looked like nothing short of a miracle.

About this time we received a strange valentine from our higher headquarters. It was a thirty-page directive reminding us of all the other emigration missions besides the transfixing United States one which were working in the Zone at the same time and for whom we were expected to find likely applicants whenever they sent forth a call. We knew as we read that we were really in big business — the business of bodies for sale. The catalogue of emigration possibilities ran from *A* (Australia) to *V* (Venezuela). Each country had differing criteria for selection. Australia would take family units consisting of husband, wife and unmarried children not to exceed three, all nationalities accepted. Brazil wanted mainly agricultural workers eighteen to forty years of age, no children under two, all nationalities and religious groups accepted, with the exception of Jews and persons of Asiatic origin. Canada had a half-dozen schemes both for mass and individual recruiting — for cooks, maids, housekeepers, workers for sugar-beet farms and the hard-rock mines. France offered a farm-family scheme, family to go together with the worker and no limit on number of children. The Grand Duchy of Luxembourg asked for single workers with no dependents, Balts preferred. The Netherlands had jobs for tailors, weavers, spinning-mill hands, unattached, between eighteen and thirty-five years, no dependents accepted. New Zealand sought two hundred orphan children for adoption in private homes and three hundred single women under forty to work in mental hospitals. Graduate nurses for Sweden, DP's of Moslem faith for Turkey, single women as domestics for the United Kingdom, farm workers for Venezuela...

It was like a great cafeteria menu spread out across the camp bulletin boards, so many possibilities that nobody could make up his mind. DP's not processing on the U.S. scheme began to be picky and choosy to the astonishment of the outside world but not to us who had lived with them through the years when they had had no choice and had lost, imperceptibly and in varying degrees, the power to make a choice. The DP's read the global menu and some took more than they could use, registering for several likely schemes at once to be sure that at least one of them would pan out. Others just shook their heads and said, "Australia is too far. Holland is too close. Venezuela is too hot."... And our Welfare organized a gigantic personal counseling program to talk individually with every head of a family who could not make up his mind. We grafted vocational training schools onto the great complex of the Resettlement Center to train unskilled workers in some called-for craft, and opened farm schools to give refresher courses to the agricultural workers which every country seemed to want the most. We mass-produced bricklayers, carpenters, machinists, auto mechanics, typists and seamstresses and there didn't seem to be a single trade that we had not covered — until one day a call came through for some reindeer-herders for the Northwest Territories of Canada. Yet even this was no problem for our field Welfare, who had sifted and resifted the materials of the DP world, like painstaking archeologists unearthing live artifacts.

As we moved into the summer of 1949, the Resettlement Center seemed to tremble on its foundations with the intensity of its internal activities. Refugees destined for all the emigrant-receiving countries were passing through the giant paper mill and visas for the United States hit an all-time high. Never on earth had there ever been such a focal point for mass emigration to almost every country on earth. Loudspeakers now had no time for music. There was only the constant summoning of individuals to report here, there and everywhere for every imaginable reason, but most often for a second medical check, which was more frightening to the DP than any other hazard in his processing. Medical was the one place in the processing line where nobody could help or hinder, sway or persuade, where the DP's future was decided by the contents in a test tube or the shadows on an X-ray film. It was the only department where the DP under scrutiny had no name.

The Resettlement Center hospital, run by IRO doctors and nurses assisted by their specialist DP's, occupied a blockhouse adjacent to the thrumming mission building. It was organized like any big city clinic, save that its clients were anonymous. The test tubes bearing blood samples to the laboratories were numbered instead of named, so that no DP technician making, for example, a Wassermann and finding the result positive would be tempted by nationality solidarity to change the fatal recording. By the time I got around to visiting the hospital, some of its workers were already in processing for the United States. In a great white-tiled room I stared at hundreds of numbered test tubes containing the blood of humans. Whether of man or woman, of Balt, Pole, Jew or Ukrainian, nobody but the chief IRO doctor could know. The DP technicians writing a "P" on a red tube never knew if they were thus excluding, from all possibility of emigration anywhere, one of their own countrymen, or a family member, or even one of themselves. Raceless, nameless, sexless, the racked red tubes were moved through the delicate steps of the major test by hands that never faltered. Even for the physical examination of the emigrant candidates, an anonymity of sorts prevailed. The DP doctors had themselves arranged that no one of them would check a countryman, but that the Latvian doctor would examine the Lithuanian DP's, the Lithuanian doctor the Ukrainians, the Polish doctor the Latvians and so on, thus protecting their medical ethics from the fierce temptation to push a countryman through if they could, at least through that first decisive step toward a new life.

The tension of the processing emigrants increased as deferrals and rejections increased, but until we had our first suicide inside the Resettlement Center we had not realized the extent of the emotional strain our DP's were laboring under, now an average six months of waiting in the quiet camps for the moment of call-forward into the breathless bedlam of final processing. The suicide was a Ukrainian who had been in the Center for twelve days, processing toward Detroit on an assurance from an unknown sponsor. He had been called a second time to the X-ray only because the first lung picture had not been clear enough for satisfactory reading. But he did not believe the doctor's assurances. He returned to his transient rooms in the Center in an agitated state, saying to his wife he was sure they had discovered something on his lungs and were concealing the truth. That evening he went down to his blockhouse basement and hanged himself on a loop of rope fastened to one of the overhead steam pipes. Londa sent the widow and two children back to their camp of origin in Bayreuth and began the difficult business of wheedling from an agency a new sponsorship, this time for a family without a skilled breadwinner.

Tension in the Resettlement Center worked both ways. Widows were made by crazy rejoicing as well as by fear. Occasionally a DP, having run the entire gamut right up to consular visa, went so wild with joy when he received the visa that nothing less than a great schnapps party could express the rejoicing. When the schnapps (smuggled into the Center from some nearby German town) was imperfectly distilled, as it frequently was, Chouka got the cases of alcoholic poisoning which, if they failed to die from the effects of a night-long wassail in methyl alcohol, generally emerged from her hospital stone-blind and permanently out of the emigration race.

But these isolated and always startling recordings on the fever chart of our emigrating population were as nothing compared to the mass high blood pressure which developed after the "farm controls" had been applied to the U.S. program. Emigration to the States had been proceeding at such a breakneck pace that we had all but forgotten about that trap we called the farmer clause in the DP Act. It was sprung in November of 1949 when somebody in a high-level place had got around to counting the visas already issued under the Act and had discovered that they were not averaging thirty per cent to persons "having previously engaged in agricultural pursuits," as specified in that Janus-faced law. The DP Commission announced what they called "a controlled call-forward" — thirty to fifty per cent in each group henceforth brought forward from the waiting camps must be farmers. And we were running out of farmers, or, more precisely, out of DP's emigrating on farmer assurances.

Ignatz was caught in this trap. All set again to be called forward on his new assurance, which was for work in a Pittsburgh mill, he now had to sit back and wait until we could find enough farmers to carry not only him, but the thousands of other nonfarmer assurance-holders as well, forward to the Resettlement Center almost on a one-to-one basis — one farmer for one of any other trade or skill.

The call-forward lists for the U.S. scheme were now the headline reading in all the camps. DP's clustered all hours of the day about the bulletin boards, scanning the alphabetized name lists the DP Commission sent down for posting, reading not just the names under their own letter, but the entire lists straight through in the vain hope that maybe a "J" name might have been misplaced among the "B"s. You could almost hear the hearts beat each time a new list was posted. These were the people who, months before, had completed the paper work for the U.S. scheme and had presented it. They had waited for the CIC agents to come and investigate them, generally a fortnight or so after documents had gone in, and when that ordeal was over, they had begun the long wait for call-forward. Very often, after they knew they had passed the security investigation, they had sold their redundant belongings and camp business interests; they lived in denuded rooms that looked like railroad station waiting rooms, cluttered with roped sacks and crates and irritable children wailing because all the toys had been packed. The weeks of waiting were punctuated by returns to the camp of countrymen who had failed somewhere along the perilous way of the Resettlement Center and the waiting ones talked anxiously to the medically deferred, to the shocked security suspects, seeing themselves in the shoes of those deferred ones and the bright dream of Neuyorke Amerika a fading hope.

The first cases of deferral for high blood pressure were amazing and inexplicable to us, concerning in the main our hale and hearty young men, who were returned from the Resettlement Center as temporarily unfit for further processing. Our DP camp doctors who had examined them just before call-forward swore that there must be something wrong with the blood pressure apparatus in the Resettlement Center. One of them journeyed to the Center to check his camp clinic apparatus against the suspected one and found that they coincided perfectly. The DP doctors then put the temporarily deferred huskies to bed in the camp clinic and studied them and the situation. We were not taken into their confidence, but one day they told us there would be no more deferrals for high blood pressure; and there were none. Long afterwards we learned that they had found a way to counteract the nerve-racking delays of the "farm controls." They were quietly injecting their excitable called-forward countrymen with something like scopolamine and sending them forward to the frenzy of the Resettlement Center in a gentle "twilight sleep" which kept the blood pressure from soaring insanely until after the Center medical check was made.

In the meantime, a letter from Bremen dropped Londa's blood pressure back to normal. Lubja was cleared of the charge of moral turpitude when her guardsman admirer from Wildflecken appeared in the embarkation center and proved by his speechless astonishment that it was a language rather than a morals problem; he could hardly believe that ordinary gallant Polish translated so passionately into English. Stanislawa sailed with her valiant band two days before their visas were due to expire.

~ 16 ~

Watching the machinery of the U.S. program in early 1950 was like watching an enormous merry-go-round without music, on which all of the DP's you had ever known seemed to be permanently stuck. And, if you managed to unseat one and get him started in a straight line toward a ship, you very often saw him back again on the merry-go-round, perhaps transfixed on a different technicality this time, but there all the same — doleful, despairing and going around and around.

The platform of this mournful merry-go-round extended from the port of Bremen down through the British, United States and French Zones of Germany, through the United States Zone of Austria and as far as the IRO mission in Italy, and it included all the resettlement centers that were laboring to process emigrants to the States before the DP Act would expire in June 1950. The "farm controls" that had been applied to keep the program to the letter of the law backed up so many ready-to-go DP's that you had to be a total newcomer to the field not to have dozens of personal friends caught on that slow wheeling rack of delay. It made no difference from which Zone or country you viewed the thing; it was always the same and always awful to behold. The dilemma was so big you couldn't blame anyone for it — not even the Congressmen who had written that seemingly sensible farmer clause into the DP Act, in response, no doubt, to their constituents' demands to make the thing useful as well as humanitarian. It was only that we had waited too long to open America's doors, spent too much time discussing how to do it while all the other emigrant-hunting countries were already in the field gathering the harvest of farmers.

Each time the wheel came around you saw new faces of old friends added as new assurances were matched in the field and documentation on new families was completed and presented to the hamstrung DP Commission, which for a while would call forward only holders of farmer assurances to make up quickly the deficit in visas to that category of worker. Our Polish countess from Wildflecken, processing on an assurance calling for a music teacher for a small New England town, was in that suspended throng, and Georgi, our former police chief from Aschaffenburg, was there on the wheel with his immense family, including several in-laws, wringing his handle-bar mustaches and waiting with the only anxiety I had ever seen him betray. Ignatz took bis enforced wait with such philosophic calm that I feared his wife might be expecting again, which eventuality would invalidate the assurance he held covering a family of exactly the number he had and not an infant more.

During this gray time, the spotlight shifted momentarily to the Australian ring in our emigration circus, where winged dragons were flying around, frightening our people into resignations from that fine scheme. In one of the letters from a Balt already in Australia, there had been mention of a fearful beast with unblinking eyes and spiny wings which one day was looking at the letter writer from out the top of his work boot. It was only a lizard with some kind of throat ruff that fanned out like wings when it was interested, but it looked like a dragon to our Balt, in whose homeland there was no reptilian life of any sort... and it certainly expanded to dragon dimensions by the time the news of it spread through our Baltic population.

"This is our apotheosis," said Londa. "At last we're fighting dragons... we're St. George!" She found other letters from Australia in her welfare files and mimeographed chosen excerpts calculated to quell the lizard panic.

We are still in the reception camp at Bonegille, being taught English, history, geography and the constitution of Australia. While I await my permanent assignment, I have been working at a farmer's, earning 1 Pound plus food per day. I am gathering the fruit and quite pleased with the work which pays well and enables me to eat all the fruit I want at my pleasure. Next week we shall be issued a Sunday best, a shirt, socks, and also working clothes. The people over here are very kind and peaceful like the Americans. We are being enormously publicized in the newspapers. When reading the various articles on us, one gets the impression that we are the most beautiful and best people in the world. They write about what we eat, how we swim and other such stuff and nonsense. Some of our women left already for the capital Canberra to work at the Dept. of Immigration. There are jobs for everyone and the demand for workers is high. Already 3 couples got married and one of our men is going to marry an Australian girl.

After such breaks, the U.S. scheme looked more doleful than ever. I had often philosophized that to be a successful United Nations field worker you had to have a little of the Don Quixote blood in your veins, a kind of crazy chivalry that made stone walls and windmills seem natural targets for a wooden lance. Now I saw that dedicated blood bursting in the eyeballs of my field mates as they ran again and again at the slow-turning wheel in futile attempts to dislodge one of the suspended families, just any one now because every one was one of ours. Never in our roughest days in the field had there been such a time of anxiety. We were old in the business of emigration now. We knew how a single delay could multiply itself as the surface break from a single stone dropped in water multiplies itself in ring after ring, wider and wider, until inertia or shoreline stops the spreading circles.

When Ignatz, for example, finally received his call-forward to the Resettlement Center, his youngest son was found to be incubating the measles, so the whole family was sent in quarantine back to the camp to wait until the communicable disease had run its course. Just about the time the son was declared safe to re-enter

Resettlement Center society, his wife developed an infection of the teeth which required not just extraction of the affected teeth but a jawbone-scraping operation as well. His oldest son fell out of a tree and broke his arm when they were ready to move forward again and, by that time, Ignatz's security clearance was more than six months old, so his documents were pulled from processing and sent again to Counter-Intelligence for a recheck to assure that he had not been indulging in subversive activities meanwhile.

Such a series of unsolicited mishaps was repeated again and again in our backlogged crowds of waiting nonfarmer emigrants. Case histories read like "The House That Jack Built" — a new line added each time, then each time returning to the same old house, the same old merry-go-round of waiting while the calendar informed us helpless onlookers that time was running out of the DP Act. On June 30, 1950, no more immigration visas to the States could be issued under that law. Presumably at sundown of that day the consuls and vice-consuls would put their hallowed visa seals back into their diplomatic pouches and go home. In early 1950 there was no hint that there might be an extension of the DP Act. There was only the stark fact to face that after nearly a year and a half of operation under the Act we had managed to get just about half the authorized DP's to the States and that we had less than six months to get the remainder across, if we were to fill the quota. Every one of us knew that this was an impossibility and that by June 30 we would have more than fifty thousand ready-to-go DP's left over in the camps, all covered by assurances of jobs and housing in a land they would never see.

You saw your comrades in the U.S. program go gray with anxiety. You saw your organization formulating vast plans to "integrate into the German economy" the thousands of resettleable leftovers along with the old folks, chronically ill and handicapped whom nobody would accept. You called it plowing them under and wondered if you had enough of the ghoul spirit to stay with the show until the end. The only ray of hope (for a speed-up) was the decentralization of the Immigration Service, from Bremen to the areas, in January of 1950. This brought the final trap down to where we could look at it, study its mechanism and possibly extricate a few of the caught ones more rapidly than by endless correspondence.

Now instead of one big Ellis Island in Bremen, we had seven smaller Ellis Islands scattered through our U.S. Zone, the final fearsome addition to the gamut of the Resettlement Center. The green-uniformed inspectors living among us, occasionally accepting invitations to our sad parties, did not seem too remote or austere. Secretly we believed that they could be gently warmed up, surreptitiously indoctrinated with some of our devotion for the displaced. It was the craziest hope we had ever entertained. The Immigration Service had no such emotions.

I realized this the first time I attended one of their Board of Special Inquiry hearings. The hearing was set for a group of DP's who had processed through consular visa and had been stopped by the Immigration Service, excluded from the States on the ground of illiteracy. That they had been passed by the consul, who gave the literacy test in the first place, was not surprising. The DP's knew from their predecessors in the consular interview which chapter of the Bible such and such a consul might request to be read in their own language, and, if unable to read, they would memorize this in advance and only pretend to be reading when they faced the consul. But the Immigration Service had a really foolproof reading test; it used the "action card" method. Out of a pile of cards telling the DP under test to do one of several things, a single card in his own language would be drawn and handed to the DP, who had to read it aloud and then perform the action described. The action card might say *Stand up and remove your coat,* or *Walk across the room and look out a window,* or *Take something from your pocket and show it to the inspector.*

By the spring of 1950 all of us who were attached to the U.S. program were like people possessed. With bits of memo paper and index cards, we ran from DP Commission, to consul, to Immigration Service, trying to find out what had happened to certain cases in response to queries from U.S. citizens who were getting tired of waiting for the DP family for which they were holding living space and job. Farmers, shopkeepers, mill-owners and housewives wrote to us. Senators and Congressmen forwarded complaining letters from constituents. The State Department cabled when some very important person, like Eleanor Roosevelt, was interested in a case and wondering politely about its mysterious delays. Each one of us turned into a sort of Dorothy Dix answering the never-ending streams of inquiry, and when we tried to explain why a DP family was still with us and not yet overseas, it was like telling the story of Creation. In the beginning, there was the Law...

Your DP family, dear Mrs. B., is indeed still with us, and it is true that all five received entry visas one month ago, including the three-year-old Stanislawa, who did not try to crawl up walls when her father was taking the oath of allegiance before the consul, but who did try to do this when the family was being interrogated by Immigration. As her father wrote to you very frankly when he first received your assurance, Stanislawa is mentally retarded; but we felt as he did — that a few years of normal life within the framework of her devoted family would eventually bring her forward. However, the Immigration Service has excluded Stanislawa, citing the section of immigration law which bars all idiots, imbeciles, feeble-minded, epileptics and insane people. The father is now faced with the difficult choice of leaving Stanislawa behind in an IRO mental institution (which he knows will be transferred to German authorities when IRO ends) or of losing for his other two children, his wife and himself the opportunity for a new life which your assurance offers. Our Welfare has counseled the father to leave Stanislawa in IRO care in Germany and he is at present pondering this painful decision. We will keep you informed on the progress of this case...

Dear Mr. C., we regret to inform you that your brother, Jerzy, was not cleared by CIC. As far as we can find out, it seems that your brother's name was found on a new security check list recently uncovered in the archives of Berlin — the WAST, which is the complete military medical record of the Wehrmacht. We believe that Security interprets this as his having served at one time in the German army...

Dear Mrs. D., in reply to your inquiry concerning Mrs. Sankowicz and her two children, whom you are sponsoring for entry as housekeeper, we have learned that the Immigration Service is holding the case as an LPC possibility — "likely to become a public charge" — a category of aliens excludable under Section 3 of immigration law. We are fighting the case and hope to free it but it is always difficult to get a widow with two children processed through Immigration, especially when the head of the family is not a skilled breadwinner. However, we have excellent character references for Mrs. Sankowicz covering the five years we have known her under United Nations care. These we have forwarded to Immigration and we await their final decision. As you know from our previous correspondence, we have a deep personal interest in seeing this brave woman get through on her second attempt to emigrate to the States, this time without the husband who committed suicide in our Resettlement Center last fall. We will keep you informed...

The summer of a new war was drawing near, but we dismissed the rumblings and rumors as the product of the uneasy imaginations of our European teammates, who watched the great crop of Bavarian wheat turn gold in the fields, saying "It won't happen till after the harvest. It never does." Once, when all our U.S. program people were assembled in Frankfurt for a meeting with a Displaced Persons Commissioner, it occurred to me that we no longer sounded like people but more like grumbling mechanical-minded beetles forever pushing their balled-up case loads uphill and never quite getting them over the crest. We were told at the meeting that it was practically certain that the Congress would vote an extension to the DP Act, that in 1949 a total of some hundred and ten thousand DP's had been admitted to the States and a good thirty thousand already shipped as of May 1950, and that we all ought to feel pretty good about that. But we couldn't feel good about anything. We still had our Ignatzes, our Georgis and our Polish countesses hung up on the mournful merry-go-round which had caught us now, as well.

Sometimes I listened to the talk from the wooden figures around me, my teammates discussing what they planned to do when our last DP's were westward bound. I wondered with foreboding if I would ever try to write the book I had thought about incessantly in the early overseas years before frustration had deadened the compulsion. Now it seemed such a sorry story.

The amendment to the DP Act was voted through Congress on June 16, 1950. Nine days later, on the exact second anniversary of the original Act, the communist-inspired forces of North Korea crossed the 38th parallel into South Korea and our employer, the United Nations, went to war. From our Military Post commander in Germany we received a restricted bulletin addressed to all Sponsors, Male and Female Bachelors, giving us instructions to be followed in case of emergency. We were more interested in reading the new DP Act than the Army directive telling us to "retain in quarters at all times food for two days (see enclosure 1 for suggested menus), one sealed 5-gallon can of gasoline, one chamois skin to strain it and one gasoline funnel."

The extension to the DP Act looked at first as if we might have written it. It increased the number of DP's to be admitted by some hundred thousand, gave us another year to get these through the mill, removed the delaying "farmer clause" and pushed back the date-of-entry requirements so that now anyone who fled an Iron Curtain country up to January 1, 1949 (instead of the previous December 22, 1945) was eligible for emigration to the States. Finally, the new law extended merciful arms toward our masses of Unaccompanied Children, many of whom had been adopted by DP's before they knew that adopted children and stepchildren were inadmissible under the original Act. It was not until we read down as far as section 13 of the new law that we realized the liberalizations were going to cost us something after all.

Section 13, the "security section" as we called it, was greatly expanded. Once again we saw faces and cases as we read. Visas would be denied to anyone who was hostile to or advocated the destruction of free, competitive enterprise. Anyone who had assisted in the persecution of any person because of race, religion or national origin was inadmissible. (How many fights had you refereed between Latvians and Lithuanians with both sides making accusations of discrimination in job allotments because of national origin?) Anyone who voluntarily bore arms against the United States in World War II was barred. (Those Baltic legions that Hitler conscripted to help him out on his eastern front, those Estonian veterans hobbling around on iron crutches, those Latvians still carrying bits of Allied shrapnel under their skins... could they prove forcible conscription?)

We did not have long to wait to find out. The cases of some fifty thousand documented, cleared and ready-for-visa DP's, whom we had innocently thought would flood the Resettlement Centers the moment the "farm control" was lifted, were pulled from processing and bucked back for a second check by Counter-Intelligence, to find out among other things if any of those assurance-holders advocated the overthrow of the corner grocery store. I had to go away back in memory to find a metaphor to describe what I was looking at now. I had to go as far back as *The Perils of Pauline* to report the things that were happening now to our DP heroes and heroines.

Our Polish countess from Wildflecken was one of the scores of people suddenly put in peril by a university degree. She had a Ph.D. from Leningrad University listed in her seventeen yards of paper, under the heading "educational background." The first time she was recalled to the Counter-Intelligence, she thought it might be because her record of "Employment for Past 12 Years" showed that she had been used for a period of time as interpreter for the Germans. I gave her a letter of recommendation as an interpreter, telling of her years of service to UNRRA and IRO and of her natural forte in the tricky business of simultaneous translating. But it was the honor degree from a Russian university that was under scrutiny. How could any non-Russian receive one of their degrees, she was asked, if he or she were not friendly to the regime? When she related her interview afterwards, her blue eyes clouded not with fright but with bewilderment because it had been so difficult to make clear to the American agent how natural it was, in the old days, for a cultivated person to move around among the great universities of Eastern Europe — from Warsaw, to Cracow, to Leningrad or Moscow — following the famous professors as they lectured here and there. The agent, she said, kept talking about "the regime," and because she thought it would be tactless to educate an American on his history, she did not stress the fact that in 1910, when she took her degree, the czar was still the ruler of all the Russias. Her case was filed for further investigation.

Visa issuance fell so low in the months following the amendment to the DP bill that the few hundreds who actually received visas were spotlighted almost like single performers on a stage that had space for thousands, and thousands of envious eyes watched those who had passed successfully through the mystic maze of the second security check. Presently we were aware that a new indoor sport had been born among the waiting DP's — the sinister game of denunciation. There had always been a little of this, an occasional denunciation of a DP by a DP, sent to the investigating agents to pay off an old grudge cheaply or to get even for some fancied slight which, in their years of living so closely together, had built itself up from nothing to a towering injustice. Now we saw the mean blight spreading...

Like a gray web spun out of their own suspense-strained bodies, denunciation of those who got through by those who had not yet caught hundreds of DP's in their final flight. Probably any amateur psychologist could have predicted such a twist in tormented brains, but we were by then incapable of objectivity and could view the thing only with shocked dismay. To make matters worse, the passage of the Internal Security Act of September 1950 seemed to paralyze the security agents on our side of the water, making them fearful to recommend a single alien for entry to the States unless he appeared before them shining white like an angel. Any denunciation — oral, written, signed or anonymous — was seized upon and treated like top-secret business, as if every gray filament in the web could be traced straight back to the Kremlin. Even we field people, who had sometimes inducted those CIC agents into the life of camps, led them around as it were by the hand, saying "These are the DP's; this is where they live; this is how they are fed; these are their workshops, schools, churches, clubs..." were no longer trusted. Inquiry on our accumulating cases of delay received the stock answer — "Held for security reasons not to be divulged under the law." We were wrestling with ghosts when we tried to trace the writers of the anonymous denunciations.

The denunciation that stopped Georgi, for example, could have come from any one of those noisy brawlers whom he had clapped into the camp jail to cool off for a twenty-four-hour period when he was DP police chief of our camps. I watched him going over the lists of DP's he had had to punish for minor offenses, pausing over each nearly forgotten incident, trying to recollect if a threat had been made or a dark look given him when he had released his sobered-up culprits. I watched growing in him the thing that was spreading through all our waiting people — a bitter mistrust of his fellow DP's, a stiffening of the face he turned toward his neighbors because he could not know if this one or that one might have written the accusing letter out of mischief, or jealousy, or revenge. On his third security interview, he learned he was accused of having collaborated with the SS when the Nazis overran his province in the Ukraine.

"Now I must think, madame," he said to me bitterly. "I must make myself remember every townsman who got out of there alive, with me, in my same time, and came eventually to Germany. It has to be one such, because a village was mentioned which only we who fled together could know and name."

Like Georgi, there were scores of denounced ones telling their bitter beads, face by face, friend by friend, reviving in recollection, just at the moment when they stood on the threshold of a new life, the multiple memories of the long dark years. There was nothing whatever that we could do to help. Most often, they had to go backward into a time when we had not known them, to places that had always been off limits to us and which we knew only as a sickle-shaped shadow curving closely around the eastern borders to our Zone. In that shadowland of their former lives they probed for the clue of a sharp word, an angry dispute, a deceitful handclasp after a quarrel. I visited Georgi whenever I could, especially after some suicides abruptly terminated a few of the cases "held for further investigation." But Georgi was tougher than most. He persisted grimly like a sleuth shadowing himself.

"In that village," he said once, "we were caught by the SS and put to work. They set us to shoveling the black earth of our Ukraine into boxcars bound for Berlin." His bead-telling monotone sharpened to scorn. "Never, madame, had the Germans seen such good earth. They took it from us as if it were gold. I laughed as I shoveled. So poor these Germans, they must steal our soil, I said, and my comrades told me to shut up. We all knew that the great conqueror could not stand being laughed at. But me... I could not stop my laughter."

I could imagine him with his mustaches twisted out like spikes, laughing even as they lashed him for his derision, taking his punishment like a Cossack with white teeth bared in an impudent grin... until his comrades in the shovel gang were likewise ordered to line up for a taste of the knotted rawhide.

Day after day, week after week, Georgi narrowed the circle of possibilities as he traced the whereabouts of the seven men who had been lashed because of his ironic laughter in the shadow of a boxcar loading loam of the Ukraine for Hitler's garden in Berlin. *"Friendship...!"* He spat out the word like a fleck of rot and I knew it would be years before he would trust a fellow being again. I would have spared him that, had I been able. I would have spared every denounced DP the embittering experience of trailing his betrayer and of finding, very often, that it was someone as close to him as his own shadow. The law excused all of us from participation in the silent struggles of our security suspects. It said, "The burden of proof shall be upon the person who seeks to establish his eligibility under this Act"; but neither I nor my field mates could stand aside and watch the DP's carrying that burden alone. Each one of us was brooding over a special collection of caught cases and looking for ways to get them moving again. There was really no such thing as a mass emigration, I thought, except for the migratory birds and fishes. As I watched the field workers patiently levering away at the human load, I wondered how we had ever been so easily magnetized by the phrase "mass emigration," how we ever could have been so naïve as to believe that once the law would be passed, all we would have to do from then on out would be to sit back and watch the emigrants go by. We seemed to be carrying them bodily one by one in that dead-end fall of 1950.

I had nightmares about Ignatz's documents when I finally learned that his case had been cleared by the security branch and returned to the DP Commission, which had not yet received it. I dreamed of his papers dropping off the hind end of some courier jeep and scattering with the wind over a German field with his notarized baptismal statement from the now dead Polish priest blowing the farthest away. The Countess walked through the dream in duplicate wringing four hands and saying, "I cannot make *them* understand that I have been running from it all my life"; and Georgi's mineral-hard eyes bereft of brotherhood searched the Zone for a man named Karpenko. Like a nightmare happening in broad daylight came the news that the United States Government had recalled the first of the IRO chartered ships — for service to the Korean front.

"At least one thing is certain," said Londa bleakly. "Nothing else can happen to our U.S. program. We've run out of setbacks. We've seen all..."

But she was wrong. The top-heavy slow-turning wheel that held thousands of our DP's temporarily transfixed had one more facet to reveal before it would collapse of its own weight and free its mournful mass. It was a dark facet fraught with tragedy. It was the return to Germany of a few of our successfully shipped DP's whose sanity had snapped either on the outgoing voyage or after landing in the new world toward which they had struggled too long. Classified as manic depressives or class A schizophrenics, the deranged DP's were returned to us one by one and at varying intervals so that you thought at first it was an exceptional thing, an effect without cause. But, in time, the terse cables from Washington stating type of derangement and docking date in Bremen of the ship that would bring the case back to us began to add up and you could see the common cause plainly — emotional strain too long endured, relief for deliverance too intense to be contained without cracking. The mumbling phantoms our doctors led off those ships and escorted to a mental institution were not aware that they had made a round trip. They thought they were still in Neuyorke Amerika.

In October of 1950 less than five thousand DP's in our Zone received visas for the States, which looked in print like a lot of people until you laid that figure against the projection charts which the statisticians dangled before our donkey eyes like carrots. The red, yellow and blue chart lines describing the ideal production were based on a minimum monthly average of ten thousand visas per month for the remaining eight months of the program. Everybody had a theory about what had happened to the U.S. scheme — except the field workers chiseling away at their caught cases and seeing the sum of the whole in every single one.

We listened to the theorizing automatically because it was a big sound echoing all the way to Washington, with names named and blame circling through it like an evil bird looking for a place to alight. The war scare that had caused many resignations in the DP Commission, the delay in getting clarification on the Internal Security Act, the need for more consuls or more security agents to handle the unwieldy backlog of waiting DP's, were alternately blamed for the slow-up. The recriminations sailed over our heads, over our grassroots, like a distant cloud slightly soiled about the edges.

Korea came closer to us. Two of our men had already vanished in that direction and in our clubroom we had a pin-up newsphoto of one of them bandaging the arm of a small nightgowned child with slant black eyes. The picture was datelined "Somewhere Near Seoul" and our comrade, a Hollander, was simply named — United Nations worker. Every time I looked at it I heard something inside me say, But this is where *I* came in! and I turned away quickly, as if by not looking I could make it come untrue. But Londa stared often at the clipping, tense and trancelike as into a crystal ball, and I knew that she was planning to go... before I asked her.

"Yes, isn't it *incredible!*" she exclaimed. "As if I hadn't had enough of this sort of thing, dear God." She pushed her flyaway hair from around her face. Self-ridicule flashed like laughter in her dark impassioned eyes. "Dotty old war horse... just can't resist the smell of smoke..."

"But Londa, you've got to get a rest somewhere."

"Oh, I can furlough in New Zealand en route. You know me... always looking out for number one!"

"Yes," I said. "I know you. I've known you since the world began." I took her arm and propelled her away from the Korea photo. "Come along, sweet sister of mercy, I'll buy you a double Scotch."

For us in the field, the great displaced drama was ending as it had begun — by our seeing the DP's individually as they had first appeared upon the stage five years ago, each with a name, a number and a special problem, no two of which were alike. Our final identification with our individual cases was as complete as if our own names were listed among the dependents named on each blocked assurance. Anyone hearing us talk among ourselves would have thought that we were the DP's in processing.

"Two of my sponsors withdrew yesterday..."

"My drivers are up for visa. Smart little grease-monkeys, I told them to keep their mechanics' paws in pockets when they go before the consul."

"Mine are still hung up with security... those cloak-and-dagger boys!"

All over the Zone you heard it whenever you got close to the people who were working, not with charts and statistics, but with the living material in the mill. It seemed to me in the nadir of the deadlock that the mass moved only because there were those hundreds of eyes that never saw it as a mass, those hundreds of hands that left no stone unturned, those hundreds of hearts that were secretly pledged each one to some single small group of souls in suspense. Every hair on their heads was counted, by someone, and if you traveled widely enough in the Zone you could hear practically every deadlocked DP named by his frustrate guardian, who knew that he could never leave Europe and sleep in peace again unless that one went safely out ahead of him. The possessive pronoun seemed to be the only adjective left in our vocabularies. My Balts, my Jews, my Ukrainians, my Hungarian generals... my Ignatz, my Georgi...

The Countess from Wildflecken was the first of my particular trio of caught cases to be freed for call-forward in the sudden upsurge of activity that began in November. Nobody was able to say just where in the monumental United States emigration machinery a cog had meshed or a brake been released, but you could feel the momentum gaining like a physical thing within you as when blocked blood moves again and gives sensation of pins and needles. You did not have to consult a chart to know that visa issuance in November of 1950 would double the previous month's total. Mysteriously held cases were released as mysteriously as the Countess's had been and our people who had all but perished of hopelessness saw their names posted on call-forward lists that lengthened daily.

Against the backdrop of a Resettlement Center transformed again into a teeming terminal with jabbering loud-speakers pacing the swift outbound movement, I watched our Countess pass through the quickened processing. Though hundreds of others passed simultaneously, I could see but the one who belonged to me. I arranged my business so I could be there in the Center when she finished.

Her deep blue eyes were moist and shining when she emerged from the immigration office with no hurdle left between her and the town in Connecticut about which I could now talk, as if I myself had been released. I knew the country well. As she had told me, once upon a time in Wildflecken, about life in her villa on

Capri, so now I told her about life in Connecticut, how the bayberry and bittersweet grew among the cedars of the ridge country to which she was destined.

"Bayberry," I said. "They make candles of it. You'll probably have one burning at Christmastime. You'll be there by then."

"And you?" she asked in the hasty muffled tones of imminent departure. "Will you be home too by Christmastime?"

"Just Ignatz and Georgi... then I'm coming."

It felt so beautiful and so simple to see the remainder of the immense program in terms of just two people, to be able to name them like milestones in a long journey and say, These two are the last.

"I'll write meanwhile," said the Countess.

"No. Don't promise!" So many who had gone before her had promised, and so few had written. I could understand this. I could imagine from my own two fast furloughs home in half a decade how it must be for a foreigner to feel the first impact of my country's sights, sounds and speed after the queer cloistered years of the DP camps. "You'll have much to do. All this will seem like some make-believe place not on any postal route... when you start building that new life."

"Figurez-vous!" she said softly. "A woman of sixty building a new life!" She swept her hand over her handsome gray hair freshly waved for the voyage. "You Americans are a most singular people... giving opportunities like that."

The loud-speakers cried *Achtung! Achtung!* and a nominal roll call began — for final briefing before departure.

"Don't shake your head," I said. "You'll be one yourself in five years... practically from this instant!" Her name floated down from the brassy amplifier. She clung to me when I embraced her in farewell. I knew she was scared. They always were at the last moment.

"I hope you get out soon," she whispered. *"Dowidzenia... Au revoir!"*

"One down and two to go!" I said to make her smile.

Georgi was the next to go.

One day late in November he telephoned to my office to give me momentous news. He had found his Karpenko in a German refugee camp — a returnee from Belgium who had been disqualified for emigration to the States because of once having been "firmly resettled." He had led his accuser directly to the CIC and had cleared his case in a single session. Moreover, while he was in the security office, he had stumbled by chance on the trace of Ignatz's case file since both their last names began with S. Georgi had seen quite plainly, by reading out of the corner of his eye while appearing to regard the wall, that the Sikorski case had been forwarded to the wrong Resettlement Center, whose name he gave to me so I could bring it back to where it belonged, with a letter through channels.

As I listened to his hoarse excited voice, I stared at my wall-wide chart of the U.S. emigration. I seemed to be riding its waves, soaring and dipping with the colored lines that denoted *Assurances Received, Documentation Completed, Cases Called Forward, Visas Issued, Total Shipped...* riding the ups and downs that all the DP's recorded there had experienced. When the motion ceased, the chart suddenly made sense for the first time. It was no more complicated to read than a motto framed on the wall. There it was before my eyes as clear and simple as *God Bless Our Home.* Our Zone's quota was practically all accounted for. More than one hundred and twenty thousand DP's had already been shipped. The final thousands were all there somewhere among the lines moving up. My last two DP's were there...

Georgi was called forward ten days later. He had ten people on three assurances in his family group. Though he treated his in-law brood like people below the salt, once they were in the Resettlement Center he hovered over them like a Genghis Khan husbanding the last of his tribe over the barricades to freedom. He allowed not a drop of schnapps or a stroll outside the range of the Center loud-speakers. It was something of a miracle to see ten people of all ages from six to sixty go through in sequence with not a delay or a question anywhere along the line. When at last they were scheduled for consular interview, Georgi lined up the men in his family and drilled them on the way he expected them to receive the consul's announcement that all able-bodied DP's of military age would be liable to the draft law of *Amerika* from the moment they landed there. With a ramrod in the spine, eyes forward and arms stiff at the side — *ein, zwei!* one, two! — they would give the heel-clacking salute of the proud Ukrainian. None of his would cringe and stare when the consul announced this new sad condition for entry. No one would look as if a beautiful dream had blown up in his face. Ah no! Georgi's menfolk would startle the wits out of the unprepared consul by firing the first shot with their booted heels.

They were shipped out the day after Immigration cleared them. They had no fear, as with the ones who, like the Countess, went alone. If any of them had the usual attacks of last-minute nerves, it didn't show up in the group excitement. They wore Bavarian hats for the departure — those rolly-brim green felts with bright feathers in the hatbands, which our male DP's pretended to despise as enemy regalia until they were sure they were getting out of Germany. The droll headgear took away none of Georgi's tribal magnificence, for his waxed mustaches stuck out beneath it with tips twisted stiff like pointed sticks. The Movements officer counted off his clan and assigned a truck, but Georgi counted them all over again as they climbed aboard and once more after they were in the truck. A nominal roll was a very fine thing but not to be compared, for accuracy, with the head count the heart knew. His mother, his wife and their two sons; his married daughter, her husband and their son; his wife's brother and that sister-in-law... He counted as if he could hardly believe the results of the risks he had taken — first to assemble them from camps all over Germany, then to get them covered by assurances from the same state as his and finally to maneuver them in close sequence through the processing. When he finished his counting, he twirled his mustaches. Not one of his kin, either by blood or by marriage, would be left behind in Europe. You had to be a field worker to know what he had really accomplished. You had to have pitted your own strategy against the impersonal emigration mill to know what infinite planning and cunning had gone into the achievement of keeping the people on three separate assurances together in their timing, so that the whole pack could sail out on the same ship and maybe diminish, with their myriad eyes, the frightening wideness of the new horizon.

The round green Bavarian hats were lifted high when the trucks started to roll. Georgi's hat stood out although it had no frivolous colored feathers to draw the eye. His had a veritable goat-beard brush set in silver, which like everything else he had planned might be useful one fine day. If anything went wrong in the States and his clan needed money before the first wages would be paid, such a classic goat-beard brush could bring as much as forty dollars.

The speed and smoothness with which Georgi had passed through the processing lulled me into a sense of security about Ignatz. His was what we called a clear case — one of those hundreds of tidy family units that our Resettlement Center was grinding out now almost routinely, keeping the IRO ships so well filled that they barely had time to turn around in the harbor of Bremen before they were loaded and westward bound again. I thanked God that Ignatz had no grandmother liable to heart attacks, no cousins lagging behind him in processing without whom he might not sail. His simple family group had no troublesome outriders — just himself, his wife and daughter and the three towheaded sons, four, three and two years old, who looked like figures from one of those chronologically graded manpower charts when they stood before you in a row holding hands. The sons were Ignatz's only comment on his years of waiting for his turn to come.

He was called forward in early December at a moment in the mill time when all the separate outfits in it were working together like a great single family intent on only one thing — to give a Christmas present to themselves, to the DP's and to the waiting world of ten thousand visas in the last month of 1950. Everything was so propitious that I didn't go up to the Center when Ignatz registered in. Londa was assigned there and would keep an eye on his case until he was visaed; then we would all unite for celebration. Meanwhile, I could watch him on my wall chart. I knew the steps as if I were taking them myself. Allow seven days from Medical through Consul, at the maximum. A day for the Immigration Service. Movements Division was picking them up practically before they could catch their breath after the immigration interview. I had him shipped out to Bremen by the fifteenth of December and my only regret was that he would probably have his Christmas on the high seas, with too much seasickness in his little landlubber family to profit fully from the superb holiday dinners we featured on our refugee ships.

The long-distance call from Londa came too soon. I knew before she told me that Ignatz was caught. The piece of myself that I would have to leave behind in Europe for an indefinite time, possibly for forever, split off even while she was talking.

"It's the girl Stefania," said Londa. "Lung spots. They never got beyond Medical."

"Lung spots! But she was cleared, Londa. A year ago when they were processing for Chicago, remember?"

"That's just it! They've got that clean X-ray to compare with this new one. There's no question, absolutely none. I saw it myself."

I knew without having seen Stefania's chest X-ray exactly how it looked. Too often I had peered at similar ones from children in her same young years of fast growth for everything — including those sudden dark caverns in the lung tissue with active nodules sometimes visible about the edges.

"Ignatz?... and the others?" Why did I ask? I knew.

"Of course not." Her voice was weary and resigned. "He'd never consider it. If one has to stay behind, they all stay."

I drove as fast as I could to the Resettlement Center. Gray cabbage fields under a gray December sky sped past my car windows. I tried not to think of Ignatz being "integrated," as we called it, into that land of kraut. Plowed under and left behind with the cripples and misfits, the dateline and medical rejectees. It's only for a year if Stefania cures up quickly, I said to myself; then he can apply again to enter the States. *If the Germans who take over our hospitals will continue the care after we go... if there will be some new legislation and new visas authorized... if nothing else happens to the family meanwhile... if there is no spread of that Korean war...* He'll never get out and you know it. The odds are too great this time.

In the Center, I went straight to his transient room. I found him with his family sitting around a small table poring over a map of Bavaria. Nobody was weeping. The only woe in the room was what I had brought into it — carefully concealed, I had thought, until Ignatz took my hand and said, "It's not so bad, Frau Direktor." *Nicht so schlimm!* The old familiar expression with which he had accepted every setback since the beginning made this new one sound like nothing exceptional or insurmountable. "One more year *vielleicht...*" His gentle crooked smile said, What's one more year?

It almost angered me to hear hope in his voice. He had been feeding it to his family and now he would feed it to me. He led me to the table to show me what fine plans he was making. Stefania at nine was almost as tall as his child-wife, a perfect little beauty in whom only an X-ray could have discovered a flaw. In one glance I saw that he had not told her that she was the cause of this new delay nor had he told his wife what that delay entailed. He gave me a quick look as he took two of the towheads back on his knees and shoved the third to me to hold. He cleared his throat and drew their eyes down with his finger into southern Bavaria. As soon as I heard the voice of a man without a country making one up, I knew he was acting.

Now then. Here it was, the town where they would live. It had a big *Autofabrik* that was crying for master mechanics. Here, no farther away than the width of Stefania's little finger on the map, was the IRO sanitarium. Here... the camp. Lucky that IRO had one of its residual camps in that town, with space enough... Frau Londa had already arranged the transfer. There would be no room-hunt among rubble piles as with those newly arrived *Volksdeutsche*. Not for the Sikorskis! They had their rooms reserved for them, as for big fish. Once he raised his eyes imploring me silently to help him out, to make one small sound of approval for his wife who was watching my face.

"*Schön!*" I said... for his superb acting.

Presently his wife went over to the crates and bags stacked neatly in a corner of the room. She brought out a box of sugared cakes and a bottle of wine, the provender that every DP kept on hand until visa issuance and then invited all his friends in to share. I wondered how I would get that wine past the lump in my throat. Maybe I could watch how Ignatz did it. He sent his son down the corridor to borrow two more glasses. Stefania was old enough to drink with the grownups, did I not so think?

I took a lesson in human dignity as I watched him fold the map with which he had charted his new course, with which he had created the atmosphere that filled the room with trust and quietness. He pleated the paper carefully back into its original folds to keep it serviceable for a long time. It was like something happening in a dream without pleasure or pain — just the familiar everyday gestures and tones of voice as the borrowed glasses were examined and deprecated because both were cracked, as the wine was poured steadily and the cakes passed around and the respectful little family waiting, after everyone was served, for the man to speak first, as always.

"*Amerika!*" said Ignatz.

I nodded at all the bright eyes expecting confirmation and the wine slipped down my paralyzed throat. Presently I got up to go. Ignatz closed the door soundlessly on his family and walked with me into the noisy plaza of the Resettlement Center.

The loony chatter of the loud-speakers, the bustle of people going places and the trucks flying around loaded with luggage stenciled for Detroit, Chicago, New York, seemed to hit him all at once in a concerted body blow. He ducked his head to hide his tears. I got him quickly into my parked car facing away from the heartbreak house of the mission building.

He stared straight ahead through the windshield at the blank wall of a warehouse while the pent-up tears rolled down his cheeks. He cried like a man who had never before let go and hardly knew how to do it. With clenched fists he pounded his knees as if, by beating himself, he might make an end of this unseemly show. His grief was soundless but it twisted his face and wrung all the color out of it.

After a while, still looking ahead as if he were alone in the car, he leaned sideways and pulled out a khaki handkerchief, one of those going-away presents the canteen gave to departing DP's. He got that much anyhow, I thought bitterly. He got that and the razor blades, the pocket comb and the cigarettes included in the final handout.

When he had wiped his eyes and made himself ready to go back to the family to which he would allow nothing to happen, not even that which had happened, he lifted the handle of the car door and stepped out. He had had his cry and nobody had seen. He came around to my side of the car and took my dead hand off the steering wheel. The quick firm pressure he gave was to assure me that he was not discouraged despite everything. He didn't attempt any words and I could not even speak his name.

As he walked away from the car he looked, for the first time in all the years I had known him, like a real refugee. It seemed to be in the way he walked. Like one of those "free living" visitors to the Resettlement Center who came into it on pass to see some friend depart, he walked slowly and uncertainly, taking time to read the clusters of directional arrows at each crowded corner.

When I could see to drive, I put the car in gear and backed slowly into the busy street. A light snowfall started as I left the Center. The long road lay out ahead lonely and featureless except for the image of Ignatz walking slowly and uncertainly on a narrow private path under the trees.

But presently the single path widened as if rivers of roads were flowing into it. More people were walking there, thousands, tens of thousands... Koreans in white cotton gowns, natives of Palestine in ragged burnooses, Creek guerillas in castoff khaki, Chinese, Malayans... Ignatz was lost to view in the fugitive flood. *It will never end!* I said out loud; but I couldn't feel anything about such a desolate thought, until I saw Ignatz again. Then I didn't know if I was weeping for him and his single plight or for all the refugees on the planet walking slowly and uncertainly with him through the thickening snow.

About the Author

Born in San Francisco, Kathryn Cavarly Hulme (1900-1981) attended the University of California at Berkeley for three years. In 1922 she moved to New York City, where she studied journalism, wrote freelance articles, worked as publicity director for the Ask Mr. Foster Travel Service, married Leonard D. Geldert in 1925 and was divorced in 1928. Hulme spent much time in Europe during the 1930s, and her early books reflect her interest in travel.

Hulme worked as an electric arc welder at the Kaiser shipyards during World War II. After the war, she spent six years in Germany as deputy director of United Nations Relief and Refugee Association (UNRRA) field teams. *The Wild Place*, which won the 1952 Atlantic non-fiction prize, describes conditions at the Wildflecken refugee camp. While there, Hulme met Marie-Louise Habets, a Belgian nurse and former nun who became Hulme's lifelong companion and whose experiences were the basis for Hulme's *The Nun's Story* (1956), which became a best-seller.

Hulme's other books are *We Lived As Children* (1938) which describes a child's perspective of San Francisco after the 1906 earthquake, *Annie's Captain* (1961), a fictionalized account of her grandparents' lives, *Undiscovered Country* (1966), a memoir of her years as a student of mystic G. I. Gurdjieff and her eventual conversion to Catholicism, and *Look a Lion in the Eye* (1973) about her 1971 safari in East Africa. From 1960 until her death, Hulme lived on the island of Kauai with Marie-Louise Habets.

Printed in Great Britain
by Amazon